The
Covenant People of Contemporary Times

A Spiritual Lifestyle Advancement Series III

Autographed with love
J N Celestine
08-12-16

Dr. Johnny N Celestine

©2016 Dr. Johnny N Celestine All rights reserved

No part of this book may be reproduced, stored in a retrieval system, or transmitted in any form or by any means, electronic, mechanical, photocopying, recording, or otherwise, without prior written permission of the author.

The Covenant People of Contemporary Times
[A Spiritual Lifestyle Advancement Series III, 2016]

The

Covenant People of Contemporary Times

The covenant people of contemporary times

DEDICATION

In Memory of

My Mom
Deaconess
Josephine Nwanyinma Celestine Nwogwugwu

A dedicated mother

nnnnn

The covenant people of contemporary times

YOUR FEED-BACK FROM SERIES II

"I appreciate the unapologetic tone of the book in times like these, when Believers are asked to almost feel guilty for their faith and belief in Christ."
Engr. & Mrs. Godswill Aliagha, Woodbridge, VA 22193

"I must not fail to acknowledge your very beautiful book sent for our Nigerian Library and I say congratulations. I share the view that one's occupation is his primary point of ministration, where he can begin to reach out to the rest of the world."
Dr. Collins Nwogwugwu Celestine, Nnamdi Azikiwe University, Awka, Nigeria

"This book challenges the womenfolk to be discerning, and to submit to the authority of their husbands, so that the devil will not take any advantage over them. I was also positively challenged by a quote in the book, which says: Give a Godly woman her place, and you bring out the best in man."
Mrs. Joy Osueke, ACF, Houston, Texas

"When you read this book, you'd just see revelations jump out from the book, and you'd have a better understanding of where men are today (contemporary times)."
Mr. Johnny Nosike, Houston, Texas

"I thank God for a book like The Covenant Man In Contemporary Times. Having gone through this book, I feel it is important that a book like this

be written in times like these. If not, you'd have nothing to pass down to the next generation."
Mr. Aja Ozogwu, ACF, Houston, Texas

"The book challenges us to rise up to our full potentials, even in our different occupations and persuasions."
Mr. Henry Omayi, Houston, Texas

"This book is quite directional and I believe the Holy Spirit will use this book to reach the whole world. A Covenant man recognizes that he has fallen short, and comes back to God. The author reminds us of our responsibility to God in times like these."
Dr. Ignatius Okeze, Houston, Texas

"This book reminds us among other things, that it is about time for us to rise up and shine!"
Engr. George Adodo, Houston, Texas

"The title of this book is quite exciting in times like these -- The Covenant Man In Contemporary Times -- A Spiritual Lifestyle Advancement series. It is good to meet people who are serious with God! God is Spirit and therefore it is not too much to expect His children to be spiritual! It is important to take this to mind in a time when everything seem to go haywire!
Rev. Mike Omeke, Houston, Texas

Enclosed is a check for $250.00 for the launching of Dr.Johnnie's marvelous, uplifting, enlightening and well-written book......!
Love Onyeador, Maryland, USA.

The Book, "The Convenant Man In Comtemporary Times"; has great relevance to our time, and the future. Please rush me five copies immediately. Thanks.
George Bolatiwa, (A Sales Executive), Houston, Texas

THE COVENANT PEOPLE OF CONTEMPORARY TIMES

TABLE OF ONTENTS: **PAGE NUMBER**

Chapter One:	Who Is A Covenant Person	24
Chapter Two:	Isaac Inherits the Covenant	46
Chapter Three :	Characteristics of Covenant People	64
Chapter Four:	A Religious Officer Joins the Covenant Train	93
Chapter Five:	The Covenant Woman	105
Chapter Six	The Covenant Man As A Family Man	140
Chapter Seven:	Quit You Like Men	160
Chapter Eight:	In Understanding Be Men	196
Chapter Nine:	Occupy Until I Come	206
Chapter Ten:	Show Forth The Light	238
Chapter Eleven	***Developing A Reading Appetite	258

Chapter Twelve: The Benefits of A Sound Reading Habit..288

Epilogue   300

PREFACE

When the contents of a book edifies everybody, including even the author any time it is perused, this could only be an indication that such a book must have had a supernatural touch and inspiration in its making. It could most probably be a message for a generation of people! That was the case with the previous book, *The Covenant Man In Contemporary Times!* The present title, *"The Covenant People of Contemporary Times"* therefore could be an enlarged and/or multiple- anointing edition, with potentially double-barrel impact!

As we know, our Loving God never stops speaking to those who have time to listen, and prepared to obey Him; so the present title, *The Covenant People of Contemporary Times* is merely like an enlarged inspiration! And it is meant for those who 'know the signs of the times' and are therefore moving from one level of godly awareness and obedience, to a higher one. Like most authors, needless state that the love to express inspirations in a written format for the benefit of our generation is like a past-time! But oftentimes, one cannot help, feel a sense of loss, where all the work done appears to be merely an academic exercise, with little or no direct positive impact on someone's life! On the contrary however, such a feeling, and any amount of resource-input usually fizzles away very quickly, whenever there is reason to believe that someone has indeed been blessed from the exercise! In the past couple of weeks, therefore, there has been an over-whelming prompting to work on the present book, titled "The Covenant People of Contemporary Times" which by the grace of God, you have in your hands today! From my experience in this area, any time there is such a prompting to do a thing, I have learned not to hesitate to do so at all costs!

This book has therefore been conceptualized from the life-transforming Biblical Philosophy, and therefore open to all men and women of all religious persuasions, who seek to know the truth beyond mere traditional religion!

Finally, I wish to comment briefly on the content of this work by saying that it is common knowledge in contemporary times, that people take a lot of things for granted in a pluralistic society like ours; and often they appear not to be scared in toying with certain holy things they come across in course of life's journey, starting from the home, where statistics show high divorce rates, and child abuse. In the national arena, there has been the irksome talk of same sex relationships, in a country where you have a bevy of young beauties of marriageable age, and of course, smart and hard-working potential suitors! The pro-abortion rights campaigners, and the controversial stem cell research advocates; and of course, the issue of whether or not the Name of God should be relevant in the Nation's

Constitution are yet other issues of concern! Some of these are almost being accorded a legal backing in some States! As it were, this country is ours to have, cherish and defend; irrespective of your race, color, language or accent; because wherever a man resides, is indeed, his primary home! And of course, no one can live in two places at the same time! However, make no mistake about it: the looming spiritual and moral threats in society today, are not peculiar to any one geopolitical entity; rather it is a global phenomenon! A continuing fruitless attempt by the "prince of the power of air" and his agents, in their desperate bid to challenge time-tested moral code of conduct, and the knowledge of the Most High God; because as you know their days are numbered!

Therefore, the protection of the territorial integrity of our immediate environment should be the concern of everyone. And so, as scientific radars and those in the security network engage in monitoring the different advances of the physical enemy, so also should people of God play their effective role in monitoring the spiritual horizon, and cautioning people on the malicious advances of the enemy, against the spiritual and moral well-being of people of our land! Failing to do so, could equally be dangerous! And this brings to focus, the injunction of our Lord and Savior, Jesus Christ, to "Occupy till I come!" Whenever such a command from God begins to resonate and reverberate as it appear to be the case now, then people in whom the Spirit of God dwells should know it is time to wake up to our responsibilities like people of God!

The concept of "One nation under God" should be reinforced and sustained everywhere, in case such nations wish to continue to enjoy God's protective presence, and therefore, to continue to fulfill His purpose for their existence. To do otherwise by toeing ungodly lifestyles, or policies will only rob you of His protective presence; and when that happens, then be ready, instead of becoming a member of "One Nation under God" as it were, to perhaps become in a short time, a member of "One nation going under" even in a land founded on the principles of the Word of God; where Covenant men have been commissioned to "go and change the world!" The critical question everyone should ask himself is this: "Is my lifestyle really attracting people to God, or is it rather driving them away from Him?" This should be a question for self-evaluation! Usually, whenever there is a constant prompting to prophecy, or to write down a message to a people, then be sure there is something serious that God wants to pre-empt; provided of course, those being addressed would listen and obey in a timely fashion. This also suggests, that this handbook, could be more than just a writing or reading of convenience to anybody in particular!

And so, I believe this clarion call to all Covenant people, including you and I, to arise to our responsibilities, so as to recover lost grounds, is quite time! Obviously the illusion that 'things will continue as they were' is a mere religious deception. Rather, like the biblical children of Issachar, we should learn to understand the signs of the times....' And friend, if you wish to live long, and see many good days, then there could be no alternative to responding positively to the call of God in perilous times like these, in prevailing prayer, exemplary godly living, and witnessing! To some, who are near-sighted spiritually, this alarm may not mean much! But to you, who, I assume, is wide-awake, and loves to see God's Will positively fulfilled, you cannot afford, not to go an extra mile, if necessary! So this book should have a challenge for everyone, to do a little more than the ordinary (individually and corporately) for the Kingdom of God, while we still have the time!

Finally, the message in this inspirational handbook has been thoroughly simplified to make for an easy reading. However, except where otherwise indicated, most quotations here are taken from the Authorized King James Version of the Holy Bible; and though the quotations may not be in strict chronological sequence, yet the remarkable harmony of the thoughts, written by 40 different authors over a period of 1600 years, goes to further confirm that the Bible is indeed, the true and infallible Word of God. So, enjoy your reading, and feel free to communicate your feedbacks to the author.

Thank you.

Dr. Johnny N. Celestine.

ACKNOWLEDGEMENTS

My special appreciation and thanks go primarily to our Heavenly Father, for giving me the inspiration and enablement to convey the message of this book to every reader! May His Name be praised even as the message of this book goes into circulation, in Jesus Name.

Next in line, is my wife and children, for showing their usual understanding and restraint whenever a work of this kind is in progress. You are all blessed!

The *Foreword* for this 3ʳᵈ Covenant series edition was compiled by no other, than Pastor Emmanuel Okorie, who has hitherto, been reckoned as one of our local Ministers of the Gospel, and a motivational speaker. However, little did most people know until now perhaps, that he was equally *a man of the pen!* For instance, he not only articulately wrote the foreword to this edition, he went an extra mile to even edit the textual contents of the book, and in the process corrected necessary structural and typographical errors for more clarity! To me, that was a very impressive, and commendable initiative! So man of God, I thank you immensely!

My special thanks also go to all other notable gentlemen and ladies (whose names are too numerous to list here), who through one way or another contributed to the production and delivery of the message of this book in its finished form. You've all done great! The Scripture is indeed true when it says in Psalm 68:11 that *"The Lord gave the word: great was the company of those who published it."* So as this book is read, rest assured that you too do share in the infinitesimal blessings of a job well done!

GETTING MORE FROM YOUR READING SESSION:

There are many who know the value of reading books, but do not have time! Others there are, who get frustrated when it comes to reading a book, with the result that they prefer to engage in any other activity, like watching movies of different sorts than settling down to read! It may not be that they are totally strange to reading; some of course, have read volumes of books while in school, to be able to get to where they are today; but bring any book to them now, no matter the title, or how valuable its contents might be, they would just casually give it a name, or pass it off! So you could see that being a good reader or not being one at all, could be a matter of habit-forming. Of course you could find some who easily form the habit of smoking; some that of beer-gulping, or other kinds of dehumanizing, reductionist habits. However, if you are in any of the categories being described here, then this chapter may be of more value to you! Reading should be a life-long hobby, ok? You do not graduate from any level of school, only to say goodbye to books! If anything, your preliminary graduation should become an open-door to the world of reading! Your further advancement may, or may not go parallel with acquiring higher qualifications. If it does, depending on your area of pursuit, then that is to your advantage because it's like 'killing two birds with one stone.' However, if it turns out that your reading habit pursuit goes asymmetry to your academic pursuit, still alright! You would even discover that no effort at self-improvement especially reading-wise is ever a waste of time; because at a certain level, knowledge becomes an intertwined phenomenon. You should maintain your reading habit, until it becomes a legacy to be passed on to your children or the upcoming generation.

The benefit of being a reader was discussed in a greater detail in latter chapter. Suffice to say that this particular chapter is aimed at throwing more light on how to get the best from your reading sessions. Some begin their reading by going through the 'Table of Contents;' and oftentimes, they try to pursue it rigidly by reading the material page by page, or chapter by chapter in chronological order of sequence. Well, that approach may be the most frustrating approach to reading. The only exception is where every page and chapter of the book is sequentially arranged to throw light to subsequent chapters, such that you need every bit of the contents to make a complete sense of the whole topic; but such a scenario is rare; unless what you are reading is perhaps a little pamphlet that can be run through in a moment of time, and with related ideas or ideology.
However, for books that have many chapters that deal with different and varied topics or detailed aspects of one topic, it would be fruitless, or a wrong use of time to attempt to read through the entire book chapter by chapter until

you're done with the book. To get more from your reading session, always try to ask yourself the question: What is the purpose of reading this book? Or which of the chapters or topics discussed here will throw more light to my level of awareness on the subject matter? These questions are important; and a good answer or response to them will instantly inform your reading approach. Generally-speaking, the book you wish to read must have something to add to your present knowledge level of the subject matter especially when time is at a premium. You may choose to read up the background of the book and about the author before you proceed. The reason is that knowledge of the general topic and about the author will add to the impetus to know more about the areas covered as well as where the author is coming from either experientially or ideologically. Once this survey work is completed, then you can proceed further with your reading exercise. You could begin by making a check-mark on the critical areas you wish to give a priority attention to. Then go straight to those topics, and begin to do justice to them, one after the other. It is good to read through the entire book if you have the time, but more important to get the information that is of primary importance to you. If you develop this habit, you will notice that you will no longer be scared by how big the volume of a book or material might be. If anything, you will look forward to seeing the next book coming off the press! Once there, you should know you have developed a very healthy reading habit that could last a test of time! There was a friend I had some years ago, whose work schedule is a very busy one; yet he must look through the daily newspapers to get information relevant to his assigned duties. So what he does is, once the papers arrive, he would scan through, and check-mark the areas that have the relevant information he needed. Then later on, he would settle down to peruse the material! That way, nothing that is important is passed off unnoticed. This is another reading style you may wish to consider. You see, if we have available, all the important information we need for decision-making readily in a timely fashion, it will be possible most of time, to pre-empt most disasters or unpleasant circumstances that occur; and that can be possible if you are an agile reader, as opposed to a non-reader, or a passive one!

The Importance of Note-taking:
Whether you are reading a book, or listening to someone speak or teach, it is important to note that the importance of note-taking cannot be over-emphasized. Some may ridicule you; some may think there is nothing to take note about, probably because some of them can easily take a mental note of important points that they are interested in. Whatever be the case, empirical research has shown that there can be no substitute to note-taking as a way of

getting the best from your reading or listening sessions. Some of the reasons include that the notes you take, can benefit others. It can be a reference material sooner or later, especially for those who have a regular note pad. It should not be considered as elemental exercise to take notes because it is one of the best ways to catch the speaker's anointing. If you realize that the messages delivered to you is invariably a product of hours of study and research by the speaker, then you would take it more seriously, depending on your level of interest on the subject matter. However, if you are in the category that is not good in note-taking, then I would recommend using a recorder to supplement. However, you do not need a recorder for reading purposes. In that case, jotting down important points you come across as you read need not be stressed. There are a couple of healthy habits that should not be outgrown by age or experience: I think 'Note-taking' is one of them! So cultivate, nurture and utilize the habit!

Dr. Johnny N. Celestine

ABOUT THE AUTHOR

Dr. Johnny N Celestine, is an anointed man of God: An author, a social scientist, and an educator. As a man of his convictions, he likes to stay action on any dream project he does not have a divine clearance to pursue; but once a divine direction becomes evident, he believes it is a done deal; and the task is followed up with a holistic achievement mindset!

He is a strong believer, and advocate of the concept, that a man's occupation is his primary mission field; and that one needs not wait to become a reverend minister, or rabbi before you know you are already in "God's Full- time Service!" It is strongly believed that if everyone would assume this mindset, definitely our world would be a better place to live in; because indeed, a man's occupation is his primary contact point with society, and in effect, the rest of the universe!

His previous inspirational book titled "Developing Appetite for Christian Diet" attracted a vast readership globally. And it is believed the present book will travel farther afield and serve as a magnet to bringing down God's Glory to earth as Covenant Men indeed, wake up to their responsibilities!

He is a meticulous scholar, and holds a PhD, D.Min. degrees; Graduate Certificate in Organizational Leadership; M.Sc. (International Affairs & Diplomacy), et al. Of greater relevance to this book, is that he is an Associate member of the Presidential Prayer Team; and member, African Christian Fellowship (ACF) --- Organizations that campaign and minister for a return to a godly culture, amongst others! Dr. Celestine and his

family live in Houston, Texas. And needless state that this present title is a book for a generation on the move! If you are, or wish to be part of it, then grab a copy for yourself, and one for a loved one!
Thank you.
-Attorney Stanley U Akujor.
Akujor & Associates Law Firm, Houston, Texas.

FOREWORD

In *Covenant People of Contemporary Times*, Dr. Celestine discusses the sacred pledge of partnership between man and God. He sees it as prominent and permanent in perfecting man and bringing great glory to God. He looks at Noah, Abraham and Moses and points to believers taking responsibility for executing God's master plan for mankind.

Dr. Celestine, Johnny observes that covenant people must develop robust reading programs of the word of God and other books to acquire empowering knowledge to serve their generation effectively. He recognizes that reflection is the master key to learning, and therefore ends each chapter with a list of questions to enhance the reader's understanding.

An old African proverb says that *when the sleep is sweet, you add snoring to it.* Dr. Celestine has done so with this present work. This book is the snoring to his earlier titles.

Enjoy renewal and restoration as you explore Dr. Celestine's foray into new covenant living.

Rev/Dr. Emma. N. Okorie,
Lead Pastor,
Amazing Grace Church,
Houston, Texas.

CHAPTER ONE

Who Is A Covenant Person?

Thou art my battle axe and weapons of wars; for with thee will I break in pieces, the nations, and with thee will I destroy kingdoms. Jer. 20]

Since the incidence of the fall of man, and God in His infinite mercy, went back to the drawing board, to come up with a fresh blue print for man's restoration, the search for worthy men whose hearts are right with God has been on. And the Scriptures, from Genesis through to Revelation are fraught with this search for those to be entrusted with the implementation of God's program for mankind. This search is still going on today in our contemporary times, because God's Covenant blue print for mankind's restoration, though already consummated in Jesus Christ, it is yet to be fully implemented; and the onus no doubt, rests on His People of the Covenant to carry through!

A covenant person therefore, is God's co-workman---a kind of battle axe in God's hands, to give a physical expression of His purpose on Planet Earth. This is a role unique and peculiar to man. Given that both men and angels are ministers of God, but angels are described as ministering spirits; and they convey God's messages to godly men, and oftentimes carry out executions, including warfare against stiff-necked enemies of God. Man's ministry is earth-designed, to put into practical application, God's blueprint for the inhabitants of planet earth where humans dwell. As you will agree, this assignment is not just for ordinary men; but for people of covenant! The New Testament of the Bible describes man as God's co-laborers [See 1 Cor. 3:9; Jer. 51:20].

The word "covenant" is defined in the Webster's Dictionary, as "a formal and binding agreement entered into by two or more persons, or parties. It is also described as "God's promises to mankind as set forth in the Bible."

In the Old Testament, Scriptures are characterized by series of covenants between God and His people; and this was constantly renewed from time to time as the need arose, as an embodiment of a seal, or a sort of legal finality to the pact. Oftentimes, this is either preceded or followed by a sacrifice of some animals, shedding their blood, and performing a burnt sacrifice unto the Lord. All the principal actors in this kind of revival gesture with God, are identified with such covenants. We use the term revival here because each of such covenant meetings usually entails a decision to brush aside the past, and an undertaking to enter into a commitment of new relationship of renewed lifestyle, and a commitment of closer walk with God. Suffice to say that ever since the *fall of man*, God again started the process of restoration, aimed at bringing man, whom He loved so much, back to Himself and hence a kind of constant round table conference with His people by way of enacting a covenant, to clean out previous bad bloods as a result of sin and rebellion of man, and to get his people to turn in a new leaf, and commit to seeking Him as their Lord and only God. Well, if you read the previous volume, the foregoing is like repeating what you might already know!

Be that as it may, in this issue, we shall take a look at the key restorative covenants that God had with His people, and try to see their significance to the present day covenant people who are journeying on the road-map to *the Promised Land!*

NOAH AS A COVENANT PERSON:

Soon after the flood, the Bible records that:

"Noah built an altar unto the Lord and took of every clean beasts and of every clean fowl and offered a burnt offering on the altar."

Hold it! In this process, it goes without saying that the blood of these beasts was shed to consummate the sacrifice. The Scripture goes further to say that:

"...The Lord smelled a sweet savor; and the Lord said in his heart, I will not, again, curse the ground anymore for man's sake; for the imagination of man's heart is evil from his youth; neither will I again smite anymore, everything living, as I have done." [Gen. 8:20-21].

Eventually, God used the rainbow as a seal of the covenant with Noah. Now, if asked who the covenant man in this scenario was, obviously your answer would be "Noah!" Because he was the *dramatis personae* in the entire episode. Yet it still did not end there: Chapter 9 further tells us that:

"...God blessed Noah and his sons, and said unto them, Be fruitful, and multiply, and replenish the earth (v.1)

Then the rest of chapter 9 talks of a fresh mandate to Noah and his family. Again, if asked, what are the characteristics of Covenant people, you may surmise by saying, it is any man of God, whose heart's desire is to do things that please the LORD! You could also add that a Covenant man is a friend of God. Also you could say that a Covenant man is a pace-setter on issues of godly, and/or righteous living. You could also say that he is a man that evokes the blessing of God upon the people! You could also answer by saying that a Covenant man, is a man who helps to bring down to earth, God's glory, either through acts of worship, preaching, or other human relationship activities. Indeed, all of the above answers will be absolutely correct, in case any of them is your guess! So go and put them into practice!

In Noah's example, he was quite symbolic of a New Testament believer: A God-fearing man, and one in the midst of multitudes of godless and adolatrous community; a husband of one wife, and maintaining Godly influence over his household. By reason of his Godly devotion, Noah succeeded in positively provoking God to pronounce the spiritual laws of *"seed time and harvest time" [8:22]*. That is it! A covenant man brings about a positive Godly influence upon the people!

I believe you are beginning to see how you fit into this mould, or otherwise? Today, what we often hear is the talk of 'leaving a legacy!' Fine!! It is good to talk the big legalistic language in vogue; or perhaps to over-use a good-sounding one, like the word, "legacy!" But let's face it friend, any legacy you wish to leave for anyone, not borne out of your own exemplary godly character, may not pass the test of time! If you wish to leave a legacy in your generation, make sure it is primarily a legacy of your godly character, as a man, or woman of God! So the word, legacy is more of a "practicality" terminology than it is of a theoretical one! Get it right, I am more concerned about appropriate application of this particular important legal terminology!

Let's also take a look at the life of another man of God, who indeed, left a godly legacy worthy of emulation.

ABRAHAM AS A COVENANT PERSON:

It is noteworthy that God's Covenant with Abraham did not occur as soon as he responded to the call of God. Suffice to say that the initial call to Abram, (later Abraham) was the first test he was to pass before the major encounter with God. It is like your born-again experience; after which you are filled with the Power of God, even the Holy Ghost. So because Abraham obeyed, he passed the first test; then the next level of encounter with God followed naturally. When you review Abraham's background, and his inclination to obey the solitary call of God, to separate himself from the rest of his people whom he has been used to all his life, then you would know indeed, that it was really a litmus test to pass [See Gen. 12].

Now let's do a narrative paraphrase: Abraham was seventy five years old when he was called and had to sojourn through the environments of "thick and thin," as well as that of little compromises, trying in some cases, in collaboration with his beloved wife, to 'help' God, work out His purposed plan for their lives!

Twenty-four years from the time of his initial call, to the time of his covenant encounter with God was like a lifetime. Sometimes you may begin to think that the Old Testament years might somehow be different from the years as we know it today; but research has proved this wrong! The same night and day that was then, which turn into weeks, months, years, decades and centuries is still the same thing that operates today! That means all the years attributed to people from Adam to Methuselah are indeed real lunar years!

It is only in Planet Mercury where research has proved that one year is made up of 88 days; and of course, mercury is not a habitable planet; so the years expressed in the Bible are indeed real lunar years as we know it!

Now, to think of walking in patience today for 24 years is like waiting for a thing for a life-time; because naturally, we are used to being in a hurry, as if by so doing, we can change anything from God's scheme of things. But to people of God, God's timing is always the right one, and of course the best one!! Anything other than God's timing is rather, artificial! And of course artificial things do not last the test of time; and God is of course, the maker and owner of time!

So by the time Abraham had sojourned for 24 years, waiting on God, he had turned ninety-nine; and to God, this was the right timing for His chosen man, and indeed, for all Covenant people.

Then the Scripture further records that:

"The Lord appeared unto him (Abram) and said unto him, I am the Almighty God; walk before me, and be thou perfect, and I will make my covenant between me and thee, and will multiply thee exceedingly....." [Gen. 17:1&2].

Note the expectation of God here from Abraham in order for him to herald God's Covenant. Apparently, for these past twenty-four years of sojourning, Abraham (yet called Abram) had compromised a whole lot through telling little lies, engaging in extra-marital relations and so forth etc., just like most ordinary humans are susceptible to. But as one that is called of God, he is now expected to rededicate his life to that call, through repentance and turning on a new leaf! You see, many a brethren, have started very well doing exploits for the Lord, but wound up in the flesh, because they fell out of fellowship with other believers, or by dwelling on past glories. It is important to continue to re-examine and rededicate your life in the light of the outcome of your daily intake of the Word of God, and/or the challenges of having fellowship with other believers.

As you know, it is a very serious issue to be the called of God; and Abraham appreciates things of spiritual value so much. So it was not a time for him to try to justify himself with excuses, like forebear, Adam tried to do unsuccessfully; because the God we are dealing with is an all-seeing and all-knowing One; so Abraham had realized this, and therefore, saw no point in trying to argue it out with Him.

Notice Abraham's mood here and how he simply accepted God's guilty verdict, followed by a genuine repentance. You see, some old believers think the word "repentance" applies only to stark unbelievers. Foul! As a matter of truth, in most Living Churches that I have visited, like the Lifeline Assembly in Owerri, Nigeria; Braeswood Assembly, in Houston, Texas, and many others, to name a few, the "sinners' prayer" is made to be repeated by everybody in church alike! And this has a note of spiritual fore sight and wisdom. Thanks to the leadership of these churches for their foresight, and implied hunger for souls! It is however, shocking that some who go to church are often carried away with crowd mentality that they are not so sure of critical spiritual matters, like being born-again. Most of them are like the Biblical Nicodemus, when had to go to Jesus, under the cover of darkness to sort it out! Definitely, it is even better to continue to repeat the sinner's prayer time and time again until this critical truth registers or takes root, rather than being carried away by mere church-going mentality, and get left out of the Covenant train!

In some cases though, repeating the sinners' prayer could be an act of a spiritual solidarity to back up those being welcomed newly into the Kingdom of God. It could also portrays an act of self-denial and humility of heart for the older born-again believer. Of course, the Scripture speaks well of humility of spirit. Now, back to our main text: In verse three of Genesis 17, the Scripture records that:

"...Abram fell on his face: and God talked with him saying, As for me, behold my Covenant is with thee, and thou shalt be a father of many nations. Neither shall thy name anymore be called Abram, but thy name shall be Abraham; for a father of many nations have I made thee. And I will make thee exceeding fruitful, and I will make nations of thee, and Kings shall come out of thee. And I will establish my Covenant between me and thee and thy seed after thee in their generations for an everlasting Covenant to be a God unto thee and unto they seed after thee. This is my Covenant which ye shall keep between me and you and thy seed after thee; Every man child among you shall be circumcised. And ye shall circumcise the flesh of your foreskin; and it shall be a token of the Covenant between me and you." (vv. 10 & 11).

The rest of the Chapter gives further details of this Covenant. It is obvious from this text, that although God's Covenant had been upon Abraham, it was never to manifest or be activated until there was a humble and genuine repentance period! If Abraham had started justifying himself with excuses, he might have robbed himself of this great experience and heritage. But as we could see, he simply owned up everything; and hence he also got everything in the package! Is there any lingering problem in your own life? You pray and it appears like it is not ascending beyond the ceiling of your house? Then perhaps this may suggest that there's some repentance to be done. Just humble yourself before God, and show a sign of penitent repentance. For instance, if you have stolen something from someone, or you have offended somebody, go an extra mile by making a restitution and /or confession to the person you offended, or whatever else the Spirit of God might lay in your heart to do.

It is noteworthy here, that this Covenant brought about a number of innovations; two of which are named here: Firstly, Abram assumed a new name "Abraham" which means "father of many nations" to repopulate the earth with covenant-oriented people, with the mark!

As we go on, you'd be getting a clearer picture of who a covenant person really is, and what you can do to qualify as a covenant person. This issue shall be revisited in greater detail in subsequent chapters; but for now, let's take further look on the characteristics of covenant people.

One peculiar characteristic of Covenant men is that they are no mean men; so right through the ages, God would discern, to know the men whose hearts are right with Him, and hand down His Covenant of authority to them, to uphold and exercise. God's Covenant enjoyed a status of perpetual succession. You may now pause and ask yourself this question: "Is my heart right with God? Can I be accounted worthy to inherit His Covenant and to exercise it? What must I do to find favor with my God? etc." Now, keep pondering over your answers while we go further; you could also watch out for possible clues in the pages that follow.

Meanwhile, let's pause and take a look at some of the make-ups of a Covenant person, in bridging the gap between God and humanity in conflict resolution.

A COVENANT PERSON AND CONFLICT RESOLUTION PROCESS

"Blessed are the peace makers for the shall be called the children of God" (Matthew 5:9)

As state earlier, it is important to emphasize that the opposite of this Scripture could also be true, which simply is:

"Cursed are the trouble makers, for they shall be called children of Satan the devil!" (author).

This should therefore underscore the importance of the need to make peace by anyone who belongs to the highly privileged Covenant community. How often you find some who look "matured" by outward appearance, falter woefully in this area. When you probe into the matter, you often discover an apparent display of lack of Christian character, in other words known as the FRUIT of the Holy Spirit (emphasis mine); or perhaps, the ambition to please someone in position of authority. The importance of conflict-resolution, and the rate of failure of many in this critical area makes it compelling that everyone should do a memory work on the very important Bible verse in the book of *Galatians chapter 5, and verse 22.* Once we succeed in doing that, then it is believed the problem of lack of applied Christian character would be half-solved, because once you have this Scripture in your memory, it is believed, the application will be quite easier. Indeed, this Bible verse is the core of Christian character, lacking in many. It simple reads as follows:

"But the fruit of the Spirit is love, joy, peace patience (or long suffering), gentleness, goodness, faith, meekness, temperance...." (kjv)

A suggested manual for conducting a self-check on this multi-pronged one singular fruit character trait, is simply by affixing your name against each component fruit that makes the whole. For instance, if your name is Brother "X" or Sister "Y" then try affixing your name against each component of the FRUIT. If it sounds sandy in your mouth, then you know something is wrong somewhere; and therefore, a situation that may need to be corrected. So let's go:

- Brother/Sister "XY" (Your Name) is Love is Love. Right/Wrong?
- Brother/Sister "XY" (Your Name) is Joyful. Right/Wrong?
- Brother/Sister "XY" (Your Name) is Peaceful. Right/Wrong?
- Brother/Sister "XY" (Your Name) is Patient. Right/Wrong?
- Brother/Sister "XY" (Your Name) is Gentle. Right/Wrong?
- Brother/Sister "XY" (Your Name) is Kind (good). Right/Wrong?
- Brother/Sister "XY" (Your Name) is Faithful. Right/Wrong?
- Brother/Sister "XY" (Your Name) is Meek. Right/Wrong?
- Brother/Sister "XY" *Your Name) is Temperance. Right/Wrong?

- Note that the fruit- qualities in the text are contextually modified. Also, "good is used synonymously with "kind."

At the end of this self-evaluation exercise, try to score yourself. If you score anything less than 100 percent, then you do have some work to do to update yourself! The reason is that the fruit we are talking about here, has nine legumes or segments; and each one is needed in order to make up one single complete unit of the fruit of the spirit. You may liken this fruit to an orange. If one vital segment is missing, then the fruit will be malformed and thus wear a horrible look. A malformed orange fruit will not even be displayed at the counter for sale, neither will it find its way into buyers' shopping basket, if mistakenly displayed. This is little illustration is typical of how serious a Christian character that is defective appears like. In other words, a Christian's character must have nine complete legumes as described in our Bible text above; otherwise, it is a malformed fruit that is good for nothing. Thus, you may find a person who is occasionally joyful or happy; or perhaps s/he is occasionally kind; but then, when faced with a situation calling for patience, you find that he or she is terribly short-fused; in other words, this person is so short tempered that s/he cannot hold it for a moment, and therefore lacks the patience to allow all the other components of the fruit of the Spirit to have their full bloom in the situation. Of course, the 'test of the pudding lies in the eating' as the old saying goes. The existence or otherwise, of each and every vital segment of this fruit will be known, when the need for a practical application occurs. Research and experience have shown that many mature-looking believers fail this test woefully. Some of them even forget that some biblical prescriptions do exist that should be followed when issues arise. Some would even proceed to make an incident a sermon or Bible Study issue, even before any Scriptural procedure is attempted to reach the affected brother or sister. This could be the zenith of immaturity, and an infringement of a brother's or sister's rights. Even going on to discuss such issues with others amounts to backbiting or a scandal. What is more, the person affected on the issue at stake, only gets to know about what is going on through some other gossip channel sources! This should not be the case with Covenant people because it amounts to infringement of each other's spiritual and human rights.

You see, issues that affect your brother or sister in Christ could be very sensitive that it should deserve being handled thoroughly and carefully; and the Scripture providers very good conflict resolution procedures which if followed, will make for peace and mutual co-existence. An issue with a brother or sister in Christ, should not call for a show of superiority prowess, either in terms of wisdom, knowledge or social status. If you notice how each and every believer, big or small is valued before the Lord, then you would learn to be careful with any issue affecting them. Let's check this out in Matthew's Gospel. In Chapter 24, and verse 45:

"Who then is a faithful and wise servant, whom his Lord hath made ruler over his household, to give them meat in due season? Blessed is that servant, whom his Lord when he comes, shall find so doing. Verily I say unto you, that he shall make him ruler over all his goods. But, and if that evil servant shall say in his heart, My lord delays his coming; and shall begin to SMITE HIS FELLOW SERVANTS......." (emphasis mine).

So taking things that concern your fellow believers for granted, may attract serious consequences. Also, in Chapter 25 of Matthew's Gospel, we are told in verse 40:

"…..Whatsoever you do, to the least of my brothers (and sisters), that, you do unto ME. (Jesus Christ). (para-phrased).

I think the foregoing two Scriptures should be cautionary enough for anyone who derives pleasure in trifling with issues that concern his or her fellow Christian brother or sister. So quit doing that, if you are still there, because it is a dangerous ground, ok?

However, suffice it to say that when you follow Biblical procedures for conflict resolution, you would then realize that the Word of God is indeed, Spirit and Life in accordance with Scriptures. It will just provide a soothing outcome that will resolve the problem amicably. Having said that, let us now go to the Conflict Resolution Chapter proper:

Biblical Prescription for Conflict Resolution:

During one of the Lord's teaching sprees, he addressed a number of issues. When he came to our subject topic, King James Version records it as follows:

"Moreover, if thy brother shall trespass against thee, go and tell him his fault between thee and him alone. If he shall hear thee, thou hast gained thy brother. But if he will not hear thee, then take with thee, one or two more, that in the mouth of two or three witnesses, every word may be established. And if he shall neglect to hear them, tell it unto the

church. But if he neglects to hear the church, let him be unto thee as a heathen man, and a publican...."

So from the foregoing Scripture, the prescribed formula for conflict resolution is as follows: One on one; then one on two or three; and if still necessary, then one on more than two or three (i.e. the church). Among the many conflict resolution procedures, this seems to me the most effective, as it provides the offended a lot of informal rooms for reconciliation. Ideally, rarely would any conflict resolution exceed even the first step procedure if indeed the two concerned are born-again believers, who know the secret of peace making. That means, from the onset, the two concerned should have the mindset for a peaceful resolution. Of course the Bible makes it clear in Matthew's Gospel, Chapter 6, and verses 14 & 15 as follows:

"....For if you forgive men their trespasses, your heavenly Father will also forgive you. But if you forgive not men their trespasses, neither will your Father forgive your trespasses."

So in the light of the foregoing Scripture, which of the two situations is more serious; the former or the latter? Obviously the latter!

Summarily, when offences do occur, as they must, it should be like a give and take kind of thing; and when it occurs, the Biblical procedure to resolve it should be followed, so everyone is without blame. The two concerned should bear in mind immediately that the objective of bringing the matter to light, is so that the conflict situation will be resolved as soon as practicable. This is also important, so that the devil would not be given room to take advantage of the situation. Obviously the Lord knew that conflict situations may arise that he proceeded to provide the resolution procedure; and indeed, anything he provides, should be utilized for ministry work because our God is the wisest!

REVIEW:

- How best can we prove that a born-again believer is manifesting evidence of the FRUIT of the SPIRIT?

(a) By doing a memory work on Galatians 5:22 (the fruit of the Spirit verse?} only.

(b) By manifesting only some of the attributes of the fruit of the Spirit, leaving out one or two only?

(c) By lovingly and patiently giving peace a chance in any conflict situation that might arise, by adapting Scriptural procedures?

- What is the implication of making personal conflicts items for sermon topics or grape vine gossips to both the offended and the offender?

- Why does the Bible recommend that aspiring group or community leaders should first of all be exemplary leaders of their households?

- Why do conflicts arise in fellowship situations, and why is it important that Biblical conflict-resolution prescriptions be followed when conflict situations occur?

- What do you think could happen if conflicts are not properly resolved?

- Who gets the glory when a conflict-situation is peacefully resolved?

- Otherwise, who? (See Jn. 10:10 a)

CHAPTER TWO

ISAAC INHERITS THE COVENANT:

To continue with our Covenant memory trip, it appears there was actually no specific covenant with Isaac; rather as a promised child, {a dream that came true}, it is obvious he would inherit his father's godly heritage. The Scripture records that when time came for Abraham to be gathered to his ancestors at the ripe age of 175 years, he gave all that he had unto Isaac, but unto his other sons, he gave gifts and sent them away! (See Genesis 25)

That means to suggest by implication, that Isaac inherited his father's endorsement for full spiritual and material heritage as his heir Covenant man. So after several years of sojourning in foreign lands, the Bible records as follows of Isaac:

"And the Lord appeared unto him (Isaac) and said "...Sojourn in the land, and I will be with thee, and will bless thee; for unto thee, and unto they seed, I will give all these countries, and I will perform the oath which I sware unto they father. And I will make thy seed to multiply as the stars of heaven, and will give unto they

seed, all these countries; and in thy seed shall all the nations of the earth be blessed; Because that Abraham obeyed my voice and kept my charge, my Commandments, my Statutes and my laws." (Genesis 26:2-5) KJV.

So you could begin to see how Abraham so distinguished himself before God! If you discover any answers to the earlier questions above, you could now jot them down, or make a mental note of them. In yet another scenario, God appeared unto Isaac and said:

"...I am the God of Abraham thy father; fear not, for I am with thee and will bless thee, and multiply thy seed for my servant Abraham's sake." (Gen. 26:24) KJV.

JACOB'S EXPERIENCE WITH THE COVENANT:

From Isaac, the inheritance went down to Jacob (later to be known as Israel). One point to note here is that God is not a respecter of persons, according to Scriptures. But suffice to say that God is a respecter of covenants; and as we saw earlier, a covenant is basically a binding agreement between two or more persons. That means a covenant can result from many things: It can result from a marital/sexual union of a man and a woman; it can result from a business partnership; it can result from a sales, purchase, or building contracts, etc. Once two or more have covenanted to carry out certain legitimate acts together, signed or unsigned, then the act of covenant has occurred! So to God, it did not actually matter that Jacob had arrived that stage fraudulently instead of Esau, (who the Bible describes as being "irreligious" anyway; which means he is the type that had little or no value for spiritual things!

So eventually since the family staff of authority now rests on Jacob, God had to deal with him on all issues of the lineage covenant. I could also see another character of our God manifested here: God's program must continue slowly but steadily through the leadership of men; and the onus rests on men to present themselves worthy of His calling in order to be chosen in this Service! We should therefore see God's choice of man in His Service, as a special privilege!

Although Jacob (meaning a supplanter) had to pay the price for his subtlety in the course of time, yet because of the Covenant of the lineage of Abraham which he is the inheritor, he qualified to relate with God Almighty on all issues of the covenant. Here, God's permissive will is at work; but get it right; this, in no way portrays God as tolerating trickery! Rather, the spiritual law, which states that "whatever a man sows, that shall he also reap" will always obtain at the appropriate time. But suffice it to say that though you may not qualify on your own merit, to receive the mercies of God, but your Covenant relationship will make a way for you. Now pause and ask your- self the question, "Am I a covenant man?" Or in other words, "how do I relate to God's Covenant?" Keep pondering over your response as we see the succeeding pages! The Scriptures records Jacob's interaction with the God of his fathers in a dream as follows:

"And he dreamed, and behold a ladder set on the earth, and the top of it reached to heaven and behold the angels of God ascending and descending on it. And behold the Lord stood above it and said, I am the LORD God of Abraham thy father, and the God of Isaac: the land whereon thou liest, to thee will I give it, and to thy seed; And thy seed shall be as the dust of the earth, and thou shall spread abroad to the west, and to the east, and to the north, and to the south; and in thee and in thy seed shall all the families of the earth be blessed........."

From this reaction, it is quite evident that he was not yet prepared for any sudden change in his course of action. If he had, we would have expected him during this encounter with God, to show an attitude of surrender and at least to ask in desperation, " Lord what would you have me do?"

Obviously, if he did that, God no doubt would have given him a better course of action to pursue than the one he set for himself, which took him twenty one unnecessary years to achieve!

However, after this 21 years of pursuing his own course of action, the Covenant keeping God having allowed him enough free hand to exercise his self-will; and mindful of the Covenant, which Jacob is the inheritor, appeared unto Jacob again. Let's read what God said to him here:

"I have seen all that Laban doeth unto thee. I am the God of Bethel, where thou anointedst the pillar, and where thou vowedst a vow unto Me. Now arise, get thee out from this land, and return unto the land of thy kindred." [Gen. 31:13] KJV.

Note here, that God now spoke to him through an angel! When time eventually came for Jacob to return home, notice that he was still hunted by his past memories of treachery against his brother Esau; and so he tried to devise some strategies to outwit any possible threat by Esau (See Genesis 32). Note also his prayer of surrender in verse 9:

"And Jacob said, O God of my father Isaac, the Lord which saidst unto me, Return unto thy country and to thy

kindred, and I will deal with thee. I am not worthy of the least of all the mercies, and of all the truth which thou hast shewed unto thy servant; for with my staff I passed over this Jordan; and now I am become two bands. Deliver me, I pray thee from the hand of my brother, from the hand of Esau; for I fear him, lest he will come and smite me, and the mother with children. And thou saidst I will surely do thee good, and make thy seed as the sand of the sea, which can- not be numbered for multitude."

Then, after the serious wrestling that ensured subsequently, with the angel of the Lord, and his thigh bone was dislocated, in an attempt to break this self-will that has not been too helpful to him, he eventually desperately clung unto the angel of God, like a drowning man, and asked to be blessed. And through the mercies of God, his request was eventually granted. And it was like a conversion experience; and there and then, his name was changed from Jacob (the supplanter) to Israel, which has a more positive meaning, synonymous with the victorious!

The message here for us is quite clear: God's own ideas and timing are the best. When you think you can go it on your own, without God, then be prepared to go it for 21 years or more, like was the case with Jacob here.

As we are discussing this topic, somebody may still be pursuing an ambitious course of action, without God. If that is true of you, why not learn a lesson from the life of Jacob here? Turn to God right now, and surrender those self-oriented and self-motivated course of action to God. If you do, God will surely replace them for you with a better option. The Scriptures says:

"...take my yoke upon you and learn of me...for my yoke is easy and my burden light" (Matt. 11:29,30).

Yes, the covenant man must be totally surrendered to God; and in fact, would not take any step until he hears, or gets a confirmation from God.

You see, there's a lot of positive possibilities in our God that you cannot find elsewhere! And I urge you to enter into a Covenant relationship with Him today by surrendering to Him. Do it Now! If you do, sooner than later, you'd begin to discover these great possibilities yourself, and live to tell the story that the Lord is indeed, Good! And in so doing, you'd just qualify as a Covenant person of contemporary times!

QUALITIES OF A GENUINE COVENANT:

So far we have tried to identify the attributes that can make a covenant man, and those that do not pertain. In the same vein, we would like to see what can qualify a covenant as a good one. Usually, the devil is known to make counterfeits to confuse the genuine; so you should always watch out, so that you do not get deluded. So what indeed, are the qualities of a genuine covenant? Our definition of a covenant embraces a formal and binding agreement or pact between one or more persons who have legal attributes. To enter into a binding agreement, ordinarily or basically, the law requires that both parties must be of a legal age.

That means none of the parties should be a minor; other- wise, it would not be enforceable. Legal age varies from country to country and ranges from 18 to 25 years. However, in the Bible, taking a cue from the Lord Jesus Christ who started his public ministry at the age of 30, we would like to say it is 30 years. Also, in the Old Testament, another prominent figure there, David, was 30 years old when he assumed the throne. Although God had started using both examples much earlier, yet there are cases of some evangelists and kings who assume roles as minors both in Bible and contemporary times; so we may not stick to the age factor here. But in case of doubt, concerning age of maturity, these two prominent examples are definitely good guides to go by.

The next important factor to consider in determining a genuine covenant is that there must be an offer, an offeror, or if you prefer, the presenter and then the recipient. Both the offeror and the recipient must leave their marks of identity by way of signature or seal on the covenant in question; and so on. For our own practical purpose here, we shall dwell a little on the offer in relation to the Covenant of our discussion; that is the content of the covenant.

By way of illustration, I entered into a certain contract with one entity some time ago; but the whole thing went in a rushed manner. Much as I wanted the agreement to take effect so that a legal relationship could occur, the other party appeared to be more excited about the whole thing, with the result that before the content of the contract was clear to me, I had been made to append my signature. However, as I looked through the whole thing later on, I had to call to suspend the contract until certain clarifications were made to me. If I did not do that, and my signature was already there, then the implication is that I was totally liable to the contents of the agreement or contract. So, understanding the content of any document is of prime importance before you ever append your signature to it.

You may ask, why this emphasis on the content of a covenant? This emphasis should point us back to the content of the Abrahamic Covenant so to speak, which we referred to earlier, as compared to other covenants.

First of all, when you study the contents of that Covenant closely, you would know that its implication was a holistic one. That is to say it has a far-reaching implication for all ages, including our very present age, and the ones yet to come. Let's take a second look at the text:

"....As for me, this is my Covenant with you: You will be the father of many nations. No longer will you be called Abram; your name will be Abraham, for I have made you a father of many nations. I will make you very fruitful; I will make nations of you, and kings will come from you. I will establish my Covenant as an everlasting Covenant between me and you and your descendants after you, for the generations to come, to be your God, and the God of your descendants after you...."

INTENSIFIED DIVINE VISION:

"Abraham will surely become a great and powerful nation, and all nations on earth will be blessed through him. For I have chosen him, so that he will direct his children and his household after him to keep the way of the Lord by doing what is right and just, so that the LORD will bring about for Abraham, what he has promised him." [Gen. 17:1-7, 18:18]NIV.

If we take a closer look here, we would notice that God had dished out His blueprint for several generations yet unborn as at the time of this message (including the present one). Indeed, all the nations of the earth means ALL. It means God was through this very Covenant, reaching out through the Jewish nation, to the non-Jews with the Message of Christianity. Another aspect of this Covenant worthy of note is the aspect of the privilege and responsibilities. God seem to be saying also that he had chosen Abraham because of what he is capable of doing in directing his children and his entire household after him, to keep the way of the Lord, by doing what is right and just!

Well, whether this is a prophetic utterance or an expectation, the truth of matter remains that every privilege we receive goes with it, a corresponding responsibility to perform. And if we take a look at Abraham's way of handling contemporary affairs between his immediate family and Lot his cousin, we would see a profound sense of maturity, decency, magnanimity, love, courage and bravery! Even when Sodom was earmarked for destruction, Abraham never allowed his concern for his cousin to diminish.

If this is the basis for God's expressed confidence in Abraham, I think it was a befitting resume! But more than that, I believe our God is an all-knowing God and an all-seeing God, who sees the end from the very beginning. That is it!

So folks, look out no more for any other Covenant! Wait a minute; if there is anything more to look out for henceforth, it should be the phase by phase fulfillment of the over-riding Covenant to Abraham, as we have seen; and perhaps the worthy vessels through whom such fulfillments would be carried through. And this is where you and I are involved! Can you call yourself a covenant man of your time? By that is meant a representative of God in human form, through whom God's program is being implemented particularly in your own *maximum impact environment?* Now suppose you are asked a question like:

"How are you fitting into God's plan today?"
How will your response be like?

To attempt an answer to this contextual question, I'd suggest you take a second look at Abraham's immediate family responsibility. As it were, charity should always begin at home; but should not end there! You should not just be a dreamer of doing big things for God, when the basic responsibilities in your household is suffering apparent neglect, or defeat! So much as your godly zeal is a commendable gesture as a child of God, but you should endeavor to prioritize, and tackle first things first, as it were. Otherwise, be sure that the devil will instantly point his accusing fingers on you.

THE CONTEMPORARY TIMES CONTEXT

When we talk of contemporary times as applied to the subject topic here, we are simply talking of a dispensational era, or age. We have so far tried to understand, that God indeed, has His 'battle axe men' for every dispensation; and these men can be found at almost every field of endeavor; and it is quite possible that you reading this book now might be one! Indeed, in the past couple of months, I have actually come across quite a good number of covenant men within our immediate vicinity, who do not make noise about it but definitely, when they are around, they inspire hope in you, so that you begin to reassure yourself that after all, there's still something to hope for, even in the face of apparent hopelessness!

If you are such a man, I urge you to keep it up; for you are indeed the Covenant man of our discussion! But if you do not qualify as one, then this book is a great asset in your hands, to facilitate your next step forward!

Some men of God have conceptualized the MIE theory; and I agree with them to a reasonable extent. The MIE here is simply an acronym for "Maximum Impact Environment." Indeed, every covenant person has his or her own maximum impact environment where you can exert control over; but this has a relative application as we shall soon see. Starting from your immediate family environment, you know all the places and environments you could exert godly influence over, as an Ambassador for Christ, or an intending child of God. Today, some go with the erroneous idea that the era of miracles is past! Some also say the era of speaking in tongues is past, and all sorts of unbelief expressed in ignorance of the truth. If you are in that school of thought, I have good news for you. The God we worship, that is the God of Abraham, Isaac and Israel is still the same unchanging God ok?

If this book is now in your hands, and you happen to be in this school of thought, then be ready to let your fears and doubts varnish away as you read on. Let me start by prophesying to you that 'Your new era is about to begin!' And by the time you are through reading this book, it is my prayer that you be completely delivered, in Jesus Mighty Name (say a loud Amen). However, you should feel free to contact the author in case you have need for further spiritual assistance to enable you actualize God's purpose for your life ok?

You see, the devil specializes in putting fears and doubts concerning the truth in people's hearts but our Lord Jesus Christ says, He has come to destroy the works of the devil, according to Scriptures. Once you allow fear or doubt over what is right to set in, you cannot receive anything from God while in that mood of uncertainty and fear. If you find yourself in the camp of doctrine pushers, then try listening to the opinion of other Bible believers around you, for a balance. Or let me introduce you to some Churches in Houston, popularly known as Braeswood Assembly, the **Amazing Grace Church, or a fellowship called the African Christian Fellowship, all in**

Houston, Texas, among many others, where you have a lot of Bible teachers, researchers, scholars and practitioners of the Bible. In such an environment, falsehood can hardly find its footing! And before you know it, your fears and doubts will begin to disappear!

Once you interact with Covenant people, your fears and doubts will definitely vanish, and you'll discover that you could be the covenant person we are talking about, meant to impact the influence of God on your immediate environment and elsewhere. And of course, the contemporary time relevant to everyone should be NOW, because as you know, the next moment of time is highly unpredictable!

But definitely, you must say YES to God first of all, by accepting the Lord JESUS CHRIST as your Lord and Savior. Then will you experience the Power of God in the Person of the Holy Spirit.

Some say they either do not know, or believe in the Holy Spirit. Well, if you are one of such people, then hear this: Remove the Holy Spirit from the context of God, you are left with nothing but letters alone; and the Scriptures affirm just that:

"...letters without the Spirit, kills." (See 2 Cor. 3:6).

Of course, the Holy Spirit is the third Person in the God head; thus we Father, Son and the Holy Spirit. The three existed before the beginning of time. So always make sure what you have is the Full Gospel, so that you are not deluded into erroneous doctrines that takes you nowhere, ok?

Covenant benefits belong to only those who have been cleansed by the Covenant Blood of Christ; and it is open to all who would come as they are, free of charge!

A SONG OF COMMITMENT:
Before you read further, please join me to sing this commitment song:
"I HAVE DECIDED, TO FOLLOW JESUS (x 3)
NO TURNING BACK (x 2)."

God bless you as you comply!

REVIEW

- Who is a Covenant Person?
- Are you one, or how can a person become one?
- Why do you think it is important to be a Covenant Person in this time and age?
- What is the importance of expressing your belief in words or confession? (See Rom. 10 vv.9 & 19).
- What is the importance of Bible Study to a Covenant Person?
- Do really believe the Bible is the Word of God? Explain..
- What do you believe about Prayer?
- Who are the Members of the Triune God-head?
- What is the role of the Holy Spirit in the life of a Covenant Person?
- How does God speak to His Covenant People today?

CHAPTER THREE

CHARACTERISTICS OF COVENANT PEOPLE:

We shall now take a look at a select few covenant characteristics in the Scripture, to see how people of the Covenant react to situations. Reality is that everyone on Planet Earth (the godly and the ungodly alike) face and experience both favorable and adverse life situations alike. What probably makes a difference is that Covenant people react differently to such situations, with divine order in perspective! We shall take a look on the life of Covenant Man Moses and his leadership roles in the exodus of the Israelites from their enslavement in Egypt. Then we shall see how Covenant Men David, and Aruanah reacted to their own situations, when David had to pay a price for the presumptuous census he conducted, against God's will; then we shall also see how a Moabitess Ruth, joined the lineage of Covenant people, and became a Covenant Woman, and part of the royal lineage through which God visited Planet Earth! It will also be important to take a look at the exceptional covenant characteristics of the Covenant woman of Shunem. And then few others in the New Testament dispensation. So let's now go:-

THE COVENANT MAN, MOSES:

"And Pharoah called unto Moses, and said, Go ye, serve the LORD; only let your flocks and your herds be stayed; let your little ones go with you.

And Moses said: Thou must give us also sacrifices and burnt offerings that we may sacrifice unto the LORD our God. Our cattle also shall go with us; there shall not an hoof be left behind for thereof must we take to serve the LORD our God; and we know not with what we must serve the LORD until we come thither. And a mixed multitude went up also with them and flocks, and herds, even very much cattle." (Ex. 12:39).

Moses never compromised what he was required to do, despite Pharoah's intimidating regime type. A Covenant man or woman makes sure that he/she is walking in accordance with the Will or Word of God!

Furthermore, when it was time for them to leave, Scripture records that:

"And the children of Israel did according to the word of Moses, and they borrowed of the Egyptians so that they lent unto them, such things as they required. And they spoiled the Egyptians."

Now think of the situation that Moses found himself, even after successfully leading the Israelites out of the house of bondage; and then on the way, are confronted with the unthinkable problem of crossing the Red Sea! How do you *react in the face of difficult situations, not to talk of a problem that looks impossible? And added to the problem, was the deadly pressure from the mixed multitude of Israelites Moses was leading! Let's see the Scriptural account briefly:*

"Then the Lord said to Moses, 2"Tell the Israelites to turn back and encamp near Pi Hahiroth, between Migdol and the sea. They are to encamp by the sea, directly opposite Baal Zephon. 3Pharaoh will think, 'The Israelites are wandering around the land in confusion, hemmed in by the desert.' 4And I will harden Pharaoh's heart, and he will pursue them. But I will gain glory for myself through Pharaoh and all his army, and the Egyptians will know that I am the Lord." So the Israelites did this.

5When the king of Egypt was told that the people had fled, Pharaoh and his officials changed their minds about them and said, "What have we done? We have let the Israelites go and have lost their services!" 6So he had his chariot made ready and took his army with him. 7He took six hundred of the best chariots, along with all the other chariots of Egypt, with officers over all of them. 8The Lord hardened the heart of Pharaoh king of Egypt, so that he pursued the Israelites, who were marching out boldly. 9The Egyptians—all Pharaoh's horses and chariots, horsemen and troops—pursued the Israelites and overtook them as they camped by the sea near Pi Hahiroth, opposite Baal Zephon.

10As Pharaoh approached, the Israelites looked up, and there were the Egyptians, marching after them. They were terrified and cried out to the Lord. 11They said to Moses, "Was it because there were no graves in Egypt that you brought us to the desert to die? What have you done to us by bringing us out of Egypt? 12Didn't we say to you in Egypt, 'Leave us alone; let us serve the Egyptians'? It would have been better for us to serve the Egyptians than to die in the desert!"

13Moses answered the people, "Do not be afraid. Stand firm and you will see the deliverance the Lord will bring you today. The Egyptians you see today you will never see again. 14The Lord will fight for you; you need only to be still."

You see, no one can withstand such a deadly and apparently hopeless situation, unless he/she has indeed proved the Power and abiding Presence of the Almighty God! So Covenant people are truly the representatives of God on Planet Earth. You would never appreciate how a man or woman can be God's representative; in other words, a "god" (with a little "g") while still in human form, until you start believing by faith! You see, being a Covenant person aligns your lifestyle with that of the 'heavenly's as revealed in the Scriptures. But notice that this 'walking with God' experience is never a once and for all thing. In other words, it is not something you feel like, 'Yeah, I have got it in my pocket....the Power of God" Never!! If anything, it is a function of continual dependence on God for critical moment-by-moment guidance! That is why the Scripture exhorts us to "Pray without ceasing...." Notice that despite Moses' close walk and earth-quaking experiences with God so far, he still had to cry to Him for guidance over desperate situations!

Let's go back to Scriptures and see what happened next:

"15Then the Lord said to Moses, "Why are you crying out to me? Tell the Israelites to move on. 16Raise your staff and stretch out your hand over the sea to divide the water so that the Israelites can go through the sea on dry ground. 17I will harden the hearts of the Egyptians so that they will go in after them. And I will gain glory through Pharaoh and all his army, through his chariots and his horsemen. 18The Egyptians will know that I am the Lord when I gain glory through Pharaoh, his chariots and his horsemen."

19Then the angel of God, who had been traveling in front of Israel's army, withdrew and went behind them. The pillar of cloud also moved from in front and stood behind them,20 coming between the armies of Egypt and Israel. Throughout the night the cloud brought darkness to the one side and light to the other side; so neither went near the other all night long.

21Then Moses stretched out his hand over the sea, and all that night the Lord drove the sea back with a strong east wind and turned it into dry land. The waters were divided, 22and the Israelites went through the sea on dry ground, with a wall of water on their right and on their left.

23The Egyptians pursued them, and all Pharaoh's horses and chariots and horsemen followed them into the sea.24During the last watch of the night the Lord looked down from the pillar of fire and cloud at the Egyptian army and threw it into confusion. 25He jammed the wheels of their chariots so that they had difficulty driving. And the Egyptians said, "Let's get away from the Israelites! The Lord is fighting for them against Egypt."

26Then the Lord said to Moses, "Stretch out your hand over the sea so that the waters may flow back over the Egyptians and their chariots and horsemen." 27Moses stretched out his hand over the sea, and at daybreak the sea went back to its place. The Egyptians were fleeing toward it, and the Lord swept them into the sea. 28The water flowed back and covered the chariots and horsemen—the entire army of Pharaoh that had followed the Israelites into the sea. Not one of them survived.

29But the Israelites went through the sea on dry ground, with a wall of water on their right and on their left. 30That day the Lord saved Israel from the hands of the Egyptians, and Israel saw the Egyptians lying dead on the shore. 31And when the Israelites saw the mighty hand of the Lord displayed against the Egyptians, the people feared the Lord and put their trust in him and in Moses his servant." (Ex. 14, NLT).

A great Victory Story, Isn't it? What a great privilege to be a Covenant Person, walking and depending on God for guidance every moment of the day! No boat in which HE dwells will ever sink, but will eventually and surely lead you to safety and victory.

COVENANT MEN, DAVID AND ARAUNAH:

Another Covenant characteristic could be observable after David had conducted his presumptuous census that aroused the anger of God. David needed to make a sacrifice to appease the anger of God for this error. King Araunah happened to possess the right type of landed property suitable for the sacrifice, and on David's request, he instantly demonstrated his willingness to let it go for free! Araunah was a man with Covenant Spirit, and great appetite for spiritual values; and he was prepared to let go, free of charge of his possession, if only to facilitate King David's sacrifice of repentance to God. And according to Scriptures, *"And Araunah said unto David, Let my Lord the King take and offer up what seemed good unto him. Behold here be oxen for burnt sacrifice, and threshing instruments and other instruments of the oxen for wood. All these things did Araunah."* (I Chron.20,21)

It was like a King requesting a thing from a colleague of his.
"And Araunah said unto the King, the LORD thy God accept thee. And the King said unto Araunah, Nay, but I will surely buy it of thee of a price. Neither will I offer burnt offerings unto the LORD my God of that which doth cost me nothing. So David bought the threshing floor, and the oxen for fifty shekels of silver. And David built there an altar unto the LORD, and offered burnt offerings, and peace offerings; so the LORD was intreated for the land, and the plague was stayed from Israel."
So here, we could see two kings, Araunah, the Jebusite who has a liberal spirit, and willing to let go his property to his colleague, if only to facilitate a necessary appeasement burnt offering to the LORD. And on the other side was Israel's sitting king, David, who apparently knew the secret of values, that *"that which is lightly got, is little valued...."* especially for an offering to the LORD. And so he declined

the free offer from his friend, for a sacrifice unto God, but offered to pay a price for the property; and indeed, he did. Both of them had noble Covenant characteristics! Great lessons to be learned!!

A cross-section of ACF Women during the recent Women's Day Celebrations.

THE COVENANT WOMAN, RUTH
The Scripture here is self-explanatory about the joining of the Covenant lineage, of Ruth, formerly a Moabite:

8 "But Naomi said to her two daughters-in-law, Go, return each of you to her mother's house. May the Lord deal kindly with you, as you have dealt with the dead and with me.

9 The Lord grant that you may find a home and rest, each in the house of her husband! Then she kissed them and they wept aloud.

10 And they said to her, No, we will return with you to your people.

11 But Naomi said, Turn back, my daughters, why will you go with me? Have I yet sons in my womb that may become your husbands?

12 Turn back, my daughters, go; for I am too old to have a husband. If I should say I have hope, even if I should have a husband tonight and should bear sons,

13 Would you therefore wait till they were grown? Would you therefore refrain from marrying? No, my daughters; it is far more bitter for me than for you that the hand of the Lord is gone out against me.

14 Then they wept aloud again; and Orpah kissed her mother-in-law [good-bye], but Ruth clung to her.

As you could see here, while both Orpah and Ruth expressed their regrets over their plight, and the idea of having to part from their mother-in-law, Orpah kissed her mother-in-law and bid her good bye, and parted; while Ruth went a step further, and clung to the woman!

gods; return after your sister-in-law.

15 And Naomi said, See, your sister-in-law has gone back to her people and to her
16 And Ruth said, Urge me not to leave you or to turn back from following you; for where you go I will go, and where you lodge I will lodge. Your people shall be my people and your God my God.
17 Where you die I will die, and there will I be buried. The Lord do so to me, and more also, if anything but death parts me from you.
18 When Naomi saw that Ruth was determined to go with her, she said no more."

As we could see, as if she wasn't sure, what was going on, Naomi persuaded Ruth to go back home with her sister, who had already taken her leave for home. There and then Ruth opened up the content of her heart (as in verses 16 and 17 above).
Men, that confession was mind-boggling, and heart-rending, and of course, irresistible!
Little wonder that Naomi had to stop her reverse–gear persuasion to this young woman!!
19 So they both went on until they came to Bethlehem. And when they arrived in Bethlehem, the whole town was stirred about them, and said, Is this Naomi?

20 And she said to them, Call me not Naomi [pleasant]; call me Mara [bitter], for the Almighty has dealt very bitterly with me.

21 I went out full, but the Lord has brought me home again empty. Why call me Naomi, since the Lord has testified against me, and the Almighty has afflicted me?

22 So Naomi returned, and Ruth the Moabitess, her daughter-in-law, with her, who returned from the country of Moab. And they came to Bethlehem at the beginning of barley harvest. (Ruth 1: 8-22).

<u>Skip to Ruth Chapter 3:</u>

1"Then Naomi her mother-in-law said to Ruth, My daughter, shall I not seek rest or a home for you, that you may prosper?

2 And now is not Boaz, with whose maidens you were, our relative? See, he is winnowing.

3 Wash and anoint yourself therefore, and put on your best clothes and go down to the threshing floor, but do not make yourself known to the man until he has finished eating and drinking. 4. And it shall be, when he lieth down, that thou shalt mark the place where he shall lie, and thou shalt go in, and uncover his feet, and lay thee down; and he will tell thee what thou shalt do.

5 And Ruth said to her, All that you say to me I will do.

6 So she went down to the threshing floor and did just as her mother-in-law had told her.

7 And when Boaz had eaten and drunk and his heart was merry, he went to lie down at the end of the heap of grain. Then [Ruth] came softly and uncovered his feet and lay down.

8 At midnight the man was startled, and he turned over, and behold, a woman lay at his feet!

9 And he said, Who are you? And she answered, I am Ruth your maidservant. Spread your wing [of protection] over your maidservant, for you are a next of kin.

10 And he said, Blessed be you of the Lord, my daughter. For you have made this last loving-kindness greater than the former, for you have not gone after young men, whether poor or rich.

11 And now, my daughter, fear not. I will do for you all you require, for all my people in the city know that you are a woman of strength (worth, bravery, capability).

12 It is true that I am your near kinsman; however, there is a kinsman nearer than I.

13 Remain tonight, and in the morning if he will perform for you the part of a kinsman, good; let him do it. But if he will not do the part of a kinsman for you, then, as the Lord lives, I will do the part of a kinsman for you. Lie down until the morning.

14 And she lay at his feet until the morning, but arose before one could recognize another; for he said, Let it not be known that the woman came to the threshing floor.

15 Also he said, Bring the mantle you are wearing and hold it. So [Ruth] held it, and he measured out six measures of barley and laid it on her. And she went into the town.

16 And when she came home, her mother-in-law said, How have you fared, my daughter? And Ruth told her all that the man had done for her.

17 And she said, He gave me these six measures of barley, for he said to me, Do not go empty-handed to your mother-in-law.

18 Then said she, Sit still, my daughter, until you learn how the matter turns out; for the man will not rest until he finishes the matter today."
 Ruth 3:1-18)

THE COVENANT WOMAN OF SHUNEM:
(II Kings Chapter 4: Verses 8 – 28 & 44)
Notice the characteristic of this Covenant Woman here: *"One day Elisha went on to Shunem, where a rich and influential woman lived, who insisted on his eating a meal. Afterward, whenever he passed by, he stopped there for a meal.*

9 And she said to her husband, Behold now, I perceive that this is a holy man of God who passes by continually.

10 Let us make a small chamber for him on the house......"

This covenant woman whose name was not given, was only described as a woman of Shunem is said to be rich and influential! Also we could see that she was duly submitted to her husband. Anything she did, she obtained the authority and consent of her husband. She made her observation known to her husband concerning the holy man of God, Prophet Elisha, and requested that they made him a lodging place, where he and his servant can lodge whenever they passed by. (The chamber of her description here fits very well into the description of modern-day one-room hotel or motel accommodation. It is possible the idea of hotels and motels accommodation, like many other observed disciplines and ideologies, was a borrowed one from the Scriptural culture!) You see, Covenant people do see beyond their immediate environment; so you may say their spiritual eyes are wide awake! And Covenant people want to associate with men and people of God; because therein lies avenues for breakthroughs on all issues of life and godliness! Thank God that her husband, who was said to be aged, believed in her queen; and so approved of her request to make a room for the man of God. As we could see, that kind gesture brought about a breakthrough to their 'no child' issue.

Now let's go back to Scriptures:-

"11 One day he came and turned into the chamber and lay there.

12 And he (Prophet Elisha) said to Gehazi his servant, Call this Shunammite. When he had called her, she stood before him.

A 2nd cross-section of some mothers, during the Mothers' Day Celebrations at African Christian Fellowship, in Houston, Texas

13 And he said to Gehazi, Say now to her, You have been most painstakingly and reverently concerned for us; what is to be done for you? Would you like to be spoken for to the king or to the commander of the army? She answered, I dwell among my own people [they are sufficient].

14 Later Elisha said, What then is to be done for her? Gehazi answered, She has no child and her husband is old.

15 He said, Call her. [Gehazi] called her, and she stood in the doorway.

16 Elisha said, At this season when the time comes round, you shall embrace a son. She said, No, my lord, you man of God, do not lie to your handmaid.

17 But the woman conceived and bore a son at that season the following year, as Elisha had said to her."

From this and other accounts, it would appear to me that people should rather seek God, and to become Covenant people, and to live their lifestyles. If you do, then rest assured that the God you serve, and your maker, knows everything about you, including your needs of tomorrow, will orchestrate things to abundantly and squarely meet every of your needs; of course that goes without saying that you must make your request known to Him in a lifestyle of prayer, like Covenant people of our study! You see, while this book was in the making, one young man said told me, he was joining a social club! And I felt so sorry for him; but by the time I tried to dissuade him, I discovered he had already made up his mind. This, of course, was apparent ignorance of Scriptures. The A,B,C of it, is that "...making oneself a friend of the world, automatically puts such a one in an enmity status with God," according to Scriptures. And as we know, the specialty of social clubs is worldliness! If this young man had sought my counsel, I might have introduced him to some Praise the Lord Clubs that would have given him more than whatever his attraction might be in a worldly social club! Well, much as there might be nothing seriously wrong with a social club, yet your objective in whatever you do, is critically important! It is my prayer that everyone would have their priorities ordered right, in the light of Scriptures to the end that they become Covenant-value added persons! Now back to our discussion: I want us to see another important aspect of this Covenant Woman that is worthy of note; because often times, some folks think have the impression that some people are so well of that they have no problem(s) confronting them. Let's see how this Covenant Woman approached a life-threatening situation to victory! Let's read from Scripture again:-

"18 When the child had grown, he went out one day to his father with the reapers.

19 But he said to his father, My head, my head! The man said to his servant, Carry him to his mother.

20 And when he was brought to his mother, he sat on her knees till noon, and then died.

21 And she went up and laid him on the bed of the man of God, and shut the door upon him and went out.

22 And she called to her husband and said, Send me one of the servants and one of the donkeys, that I may go quickly to the man of God and come back again.

23 And he said, Why go to him today? It is neither the New Moon nor the Sabbath. And she said, It will be all right."

From all indications here, it would appear like this woman was the go-getter of the house; but even then, she was so godly, that she would do nothing until she gets her husband's approval and blessing! This is amazing! So, she got all that done, she took off like a warrior! Indeed Covenant people are spiritual warriors! Then let's see the rest of the story:-

"24 Then she saddled the donkey and said to her servant, Ride fast; do not slacken your pace for me unless I tell you.

25 So she set out and came to the man of God at Mount Carmel. When the man of God saw her afar off, he said to Gehazi his servant, Behold, yonder is that Shunammite.

26 Run to meet her and say, Is it well with you? Well with your husband? Well with the child? And she answered, It is well."

Now she sped to the location of the man of God, Elisha. And apparently, she had made up her mind to unburden her heart to none other than the man of God, Prophet Elisha himself. Little wonder that when Elisha's servant asked her 'Is it well?" She simply replied, "It is well;" even though the reverse was absolutely the case! You could see a lioness at heart in terms of resilence! Let's read further:-

"27 When she came to the mountain to the man of God, she clung to his feet. Gehazi came to thrust her away, but the man of God said, Let her alone, for her soul is bitter and vexed within her, and the Lord has hid it from me and has not told me.

28 Then she said, Did I desire a son of my lord? Did I not say, Do not deceive me?"

Notice that once she was at the right place, she fell down, and unburdened her heart to the man of God. Today, when seeking a solution to some problems, people go about it anyhow, until everybody hears about it to form a "Pity Party!" And of course we know that Pity Parties are never known to solve any problem! Only God, or real men of God can meaningfully and prayerfully feel your pain, and be able to take it up prayerfully. So let us learn something from the lifestyle of Covenant people of our discussion. Once this lesson is learned, we will have less problems in families, and in effect, in churches; because most people will become problem-solvers! And in so doing, the devil will rendered jobless, and sent packing out of our vicinity, to the glory of God!

"29 Then he said to Gehazi, Gird up your loins and take my staff in your hand and go lay my staff on the face of the child. If you meet any man, do not salute him. If he salutes you, do not answer him.

30 The mother of the child said, As the Lord lives and as my soul lives, I will not leave you. And he arose and followed her."

As we could see from the foregoing, once the woman has reached her destination, even the place of the man of God, Prophet Elisha, she would not let go, until she got a first-hand attention from the man of God. So she humbly, but resolutely held her grip on the man of God of course, for a critical intervention in an apparently hopeless situation, humanly speaking; because as we could see, the child is not merely sick, but already dead! At such a exercise of faith, the man of God had to get up and go with her to attend to the situation!

31 Gehazi passed on before them and laid the staff on the child's face, but the boy neither spoke nor heard. So he went back to meet Elisha and said to him, The child has not awakened.

32 When Elisha arrived in the house, the child was dead and laid upon his bed.

33 So he went in, shut the door on the two of them, and prayed to the Lord.

34 He went up and lay on the child, put his mouth on his mouth, his eyes on his eyes, and his hands on his hands. And as he stretched himself on him and embraced him, the child's flesh became warm.

35 Then he returned and walked in the house to and fro and went up again and stretched himself upon him. And the child sneezed seven times, and then opened his eyes.

36 Then [Elisha] called Gehazi and said, Call this Shunammite. So he called her. And when she came, he said, 'Take up your son.'

37 She came and fell at his feet, bowing herself to the ground. Then she took up her son and went out. (AMP)."

Thank God the child came back to life! So I don't know what your own situation might be today; May be hopeless, or maybe not as hopeless as this, but one thing is sure: A Covenant approach can solve any problem; because a covenant lifestyle realizes that God made us for His own pleasure, and wants the best for you, provided of course, you have acknowledged him as your Lord and Savior. You should also realize the importance of prayer as a spiritual tool, and the divine command that we should *"Pray without ceasing."*

Praise the Lord!

THE COVENANT PERSON, JOSEPH OF ARIMATHEA:

The Burial of Jesus (Matt. 27:NLT)

[57] As evening approached, Joseph, a rich man from Arimathea who had become a follower of Jesus, [58] went to Pilate and asked for Jesus' body. And Pilate issued an order to release it to him. [59] Joseph took the body and wrapped it in a long sheet of clean linen cloth. [60] He placed it in his own new tomb, which had been carved out of the rock. Then he rolled a great stone across the entrance and left. [61] Both Mary Magdalene and the other Mary were sitting across from the tomb and watching.

You see, a Covenant person would do everything, but toy with holy things; you could do all the games you wish with them, but when it comes to that, a man or woman of covenant would either tactically quit the environment, or freeze out from the conversation. The reason is obvious: Therein lies his or her covenant substance. If you learned the secret of telling the truth for instance, you would realize a little of what is being said here. Any time you tell the truth, especially when it is inconvenient to do so, or perhaps when a little lie would have 'hurt no one' then something divine will drop into your system! It is usually like the Spirit of God, or an angelic touch, patting you on the back and saying, 'Yes, you are one of Mine!' And at that moment, you are filled with a sense of integrity, or inner strength! So here comes Covenant Man, Joseph of Arimathea, whom many have accused of being a secret disciple! Yet at this point, he did not hesitate to identify with his Lord and Savior, even at his death: He proceeded to demand the Lord's body from the authorities, so he could give Him a decent and befitting burial!

THE COVENANT WOMEN, MARY MAGDALENE & THE OTHER MARY:

The Resurrection

28 Early on Sunday morning,[o] as the new day was dawning, Mary Magdalene and the other Mary went out to visit the tomb.

(Matt. 28:NLT)

² Suddenly there was a great earthquake! For an angel of the Lord came down from heaven, rolled aside the stone, and sat on it. ³ His face shone like lightning, and his clothing was as white as snow. ⁴ The guards shook with fear when they saw him, and they fell into a dead faint.

⁵ Then the angel spoke to the women. "Don't be afraid!" he said. "I know you are looking for Jesus, who was crucified. ⁶ He isn't here! He is risen from the dead, just as he said would happen. Come, see where his body was lying. ⁷ And now, go quickly and tell his disciples that he has risen from the dead, and he is going ahead of you to Galilee. You will see him there. Remember what I have told you."

⁸ The women ran quickly from the tomb. They were very frightened but also filled with great joy, and they rushed to give the disciples the angel's message. ⁹ And as they went, Jesus met them and greeted them. And they ran to him, grasped his feet, and worshiped him. ¹⁰ Then Jesus said to them, "Don't be afraid! Go tell my brothers to leave for Galilee, and they will see me there."

To non-committed people of the world, once the source of miracle, wealth, or anything of pleasant surprise, is no more active, then that is the end of the game! But not so with Covenant people. For Covenant Woman Mary and her namesake, they knew that even though it appears to be all over, yet it could the beginning a greater miracle yet to be experienced, based on their belief and faith on the spoken Word of God. So after the crowd had parted ways, they planned a visit to the holy tomb, where the Lord was laid. And there commitment paid off! They became the very first to behold the 'Risen Lord' and the miracle of resurrection! Of course, don't ever expect to be used of God, for any significant task, unless and until He sees the Mark of the Covenant in you. And of course, getting this mark, is a spiritual phenomenon. Let me use one Scriptural passage to diffuse it: Romans chapter 10, verses 9 and 10 reads:

⁹ ...... if you confess with your mouth the Lord Jesus and believe in your heart that God has raised Him from the dead, you will be saved. ¹⁰ For with the heart one believes unto righteousness, and with the mouth confession is made unto salvation.(New KJV).

Another cross-section of Mothers' Day Celebrations at African Christian Fellowship, in Houston, Texas.(3)

This is the critical first step to becoming a Covenant Person! So go ahead, take it, and let's go from there!

To cap up, although research and experience do show that there are indeed, a lot of living contemporary saints walking the face of the earth today, yet it is not the objective of this book to attempt naming names like was attempted in the previous edition. The reason is obvious---to forestall the temptation of anyone so named, being filled with a sense of complacency, or flattered, as it were. If anything, the challenge this book seeks to put across is that all who have embraced the covenant principles, should by their exemplary lifestyles, seek to bring more people to the saving knowledge of God, through our Lord Jesus Christ, so that together, everyone would rejoice that "our names have been written in the book of Life!" There can be no greater spiritual value or achievement than that!

Review:
The Characteristics of Covenant People:

- Name some of the critical characteristics of Covenant people? (Ratings: 3-5 characteristics = Good). (4-6=Excellent). (7-10 = Outstanding)

- What in your opinion, made Moses' approach to issues different?
- What do you think, made King David and Araunah's case peculiar?
- Compare and contrast between king Arauanh free will disposition with his property in our text, and Neboth's tight-fist approach with his. (I Kings 21).
- If an intruder confronts you and says "Your property or your life...." How will you react?
- What peculiar characteristics did the Covenant Woman of Shunem manifest that are worthy of emulation by today's Christian women?
- From her husband's reaction to the situation, do you think he was a believer?
- From what you learned in this chapter, how would you handle your own life issues?
- What role do you think God expects us to play if and when there is a problem in our lives or family?
- Do you believe the dead can still be brought back to life today?

CHAPTER FOUR

A RELIGIOUS OFFICER JOINS THE COVENANT TRAIN!

The Scripture is fraught with many religious persons from different backgrounds, who encountered "Help from Above" and became covenant persons. The case of one-time Saul, changed to Paul, whose belligerent conviction made him see killing of believers as a service to his gods, was discussed in one of my books titled "Team Players for a Worthy Goal."

In this particular study, we shall be dissecting, in an attempt to digest another brand of religious man, who was not only philanthropic, he was equally reckoned as being prayerful and God-fearing. Apparently his was so exceptional that God had to dispatch an angel to show him how to go about embracing 'Help from Above' which he had sought so much through various religious practices! A Muslim co-worker who is liberal with his material possessions, and quite keen to help needy friends around him, was fascinated when I told him how God sent an angel unto liberal Cornelius, to show him the way of salvation. So the picture of Cornelius here, could embody the ideals of most religious practices;

that mean a Muslim, or a Hindu, or a Roman Catholic, Judaism religion to name a few, could fit into his picture. Why, you may ask! And the obvious reason is that most religious persuasions do aim to practice what Cornelius is known to be doing before his encounter with 'Help from Above,' as is evident in the Scripture that follow:
Cornelius Calls Peter:

"In Ceasarea, there lived a Roman army officer, named Cornelius who was a captain of the Italian Regiment. He was a devout God-fearing man, as was everyone in his house hold. He gave generously to the poor, and prayed regularly to God."

Let's pause here to attempt a match of this man's characteristics in relation to some religions. Aside from Cornelius' regimental status as a captain, this man is described as a devout God-fearing man. Reputable gentlemen and ladies of the Muslim religion are often described *as devout Muslims*; and of course, they believe a lot in giving alms to the poor and needy, and they are also associated with praying five times a day, facing the sun! Catholics likewise pray using their beads or chaplets. This brings to mind a visitor friend I had the opportunity to host some time ago. This friend had come in company of his parents, who were good Catholics. Time came to bless something to eat and drink, and the elderly Papa was requested to do the praying; and instantly, my friend's dad got on board! He offered Hail Mary, several times; Our Lord's Prayer, several times, and other subordinate Catholic prayers, several times. Men, for about 30 minutes we were subjected to a duel of repetitive prayers, and no one could say, stop! Thanks for the timely intervention of the man's wife, who promptly cut in with another version of prayer, and then tactically brought the prayer session to an end! So some Roman Catholics do show their religious devotion through rote prayer; as well as in doing good, and giving of alms. Other religions believe only in goodness and well-being right here and now, and no significant expectation of life after death, like the Hindi. Of course, the Christian faith, which is popularly known as a religion of relationship and love, believes in the vertical and a horizontal relationships to God and man respectively. On a more serious note, one Scripture stands out clearly in support of interpersonal relationships.

It says: *"...If you do not love your brother whom you see, how can you love God whom you do not see...."* (I John 4:20 – Para-phrased).

The important point that should be noted here, is that if Cornelius was ok doing just what he was doing religiously, then there might have been no need to get further "Help from Above" as announced to him by the angelic visitor from the Presence of God. This clearly places CHRISTIANITY above all man-made religions. And once you welcome Jesus Christ (God's sent Help from above) into your heart, as your Lord and Savior, you secure a passport to heaven, like Captain Cornelius of our text; so that when your life on Planet Earth ends, you can have access to heaven.

To get a full gist of Cornelius's encounter with the heavenly visitor, and for emphasis, let's read a little further from Scripture:

"One afternoon, about three o'clock, he (Cornelius) had a vision in which he saw an angel of God coming toward him. "Cornelius," the angel sad. Cornelius stared at him in terror. "What is it Sir," he asked the angel. And the Angel replied, "Your prayers and gifts to the poor have been received by God as an offering. Now send some men to Joppa and summon a man named Simon Peter. He is staying with Simon the tanner, who lives near the sea shore."

As soon as the angel was gone, Cornelius called two of his household servants and a devout soldier, one of his personal attendants. He told them what had happened, and sent them off to Joppa.

Peter Visits Cornelius:

The next day as Cornelius' messengers were nearing the town, Peter went up on the flat roof to pray. It was about noon, and he was hungry. But while a meal was being prepared, he fell into a trance. He saw the sky open and something like a large sheet was let down by its four corners. In the sheet were all sorts of animals, reptiles, and birds. Then a voice said to him, "Get up, Peter; kill and eat them." "No Lord," Peter declared, "I have never eaten anything that our Jewish laws have declared impure and unclean." But the voice spoke again: "Do not call something unclean if God has made it clean." The same vision was repeated three times. Then the sheet was suddenly pulled up to heaven.

Peter was very perplexed! What could the visions mean? Just then, the men sent by Cornelius found Simon's house. Standing outside the gate, they asked if a man named Simon Peter was staying there. Meanwhile, as Peter was puzzling over the vision, the Holy Spirit said to him, "Three men have come looking for you. Get up, go downstairs and go with them without hesitation. Don't worry for I have sent them. So Peter went down and said "I am the man you are looking for. Why have you come?" They said "We were sent by Cornelius, a Roman Officer. He is a devout and God-

fearing man, well respected by all the Jews. A holy angel instructed him to summon you to his house so that he can hear your message. So Peter invited the men to stay for the night. The next day, he went with them, accompanied by some of the brothers from Joppa. They arrived in Ceasarea the following day. Cornelius was waiting for them, and had called together his relatives and close friends. As Peter entered his home, Cornelius fell at his feet and worshipped him. But Peter pulled him up and said "Stand up! I'm a human being just like you!" So they talked together and went inside where many others were assembled."

You see, some would be scared to death if they happen to see an angel appear to them, not to talk of having the courage to hear what he has to say. Although Cornelius was scared at the sight of this angel of God, yet he summoned courage to catch the message the angel came to deliver to him. And of course, once he grabbed it, he never hesitated to pursue the course of the heavenly message, indeed, like the remaining of his lifespan hinged on that message! Of course, in actual fact, his remaining life on earth would depend on what he did with the crucial heavenly message. As we know, once you pay due attention to heavenly matters other issues of life fall in line. This is consistent with Scriptures. (See Proverbs 14 verse 34 which says *"Godliness exalts a nation...."*

By extension, godliness is the watchword for real success in life and there is no talk of godliness unless you have embraced the reality of "Help from Above" as already explained above. And as we know, your reaction to "Help from Above" will determine where you will spend our eternity---heaven or hell. But the good news is that you are reading this book because someone cares, and wishes that every reader should make it to heaven when life on Planet Earth is over. If you agree then declare it by saying: Oh God, Forgive me my sins; I welcome Jesus Christ into my life as my Lord and Savior right now. Please make me truly thine, in Jesus Name. Amen!

Finally, like Cornelius, begin to take your dreams and visions more seriously, because some of them are God's privileged information for your edification. So if you have been passive about the messages you receive from God, either through dreams or visions, or even from earth-bound ministers of God, who tell you about "Help from Above" for all mankind then this is the time to change that attitude, because our heavenly Father is loving, and does not want anyone to perish through ignorance, or unbelief.

The bottom line about former good, moralist, religious Cornelius is that he took the angelic message seriously, pursued the course of the message, and then received the Gospel, and he, his family and invited friends were born again and they received the gift of the Holy Spirit, and were baptized; and thus they instantly became heavenly candidates. So while the door is still open, you too can have Cornelius' type of experience. When we talk of Covenant People of Contemporary Times, that is what we are talking about!

THE PLACE OF PRAYER FOR COVENANT PEOPLE

Captain Cornelius of our above text, was described as a prayerful man. Yet even as a military officer, he never chose to answer "Prayer Warrior" to his name! If being religious alone was enough to get people into heaven, I believe Cornelius would have made it; because he was in every way religious, and quite humble about it! No wonder that God took notice of him, and showed him the way to the Kingdom of God --- Jesus Christ!

Often times, those who take advantage of the privilege of prayer are referred to as Prayer Warriors. Well there are few things that need to be said about the two little words, "Prayer" and "Warrior." Firstly, prayer does not have a dual universal English Language usage; otherwise, it should have been able to stand on its own as "Prayer" on the one hand, while the person who prayed, on the other hand, is equally referred to as "a Prayer." Therefore, because of this language lapse, the word "Warrior" became a conducive addition, to qualify the man or woman who engages in the warfare of prayer.

To define the two words together the words prayer warrior should mean the person who does warfare in prayer. This new terminology as it were, had better be used merely in descriptive terms to define the *dramatis personae* involved in the act of praying, as opposed to a titular terminology. Obviously, no one who understands the dynamics of prayer would like to be called by such a bogus title. As we learn from Scriptures, prayer is a privilege made available to born again believers in Christ, for the purpose of communicating their needs to their Heavenly Father. Indeed, it is an exclusive privilege to believers; that is why the Scriptures describe the prayer of non-believers, as an abomination.... On the other hand, it states that "God's ears are open to His children's prayers....." What a privilege! If you make a constant recourse to the privilege of prayer, then we would realize, and conclude that you are indeed, doing yourself a lot of favors! Personally, if I talk to my Heavenly Father, like I constantly do, concerning my many issues and needs, or perhaps I join someone to pray about their needs, and our prayers are answered as is constantly the case, then I don't need anybody calling me a prayer warrior's name or title. So such a title is one of the many cheap offers that believers should politely and humbly decline. Even if you constantly pray for other people and they are blessed, it still should not qualify you for a prayer warrior title. So everyone should be humble enough to realize that things of spiritual value do not call for a big title branding because such big titles could constitute a hindrance to the flow of the Holy Spirit in many ways. The praying believer should rather give all the glory to God when he is used to accomplish any spiritual feat; because without Him, you can do nothing, as it were! Otherwise, anyone who prefers ambitious moves to be popular by taking bogus titles, should realize that this amounts to taking the glory that is due to God; and such a move could only be the beginning of an end of such a ministry! The lifestyle and ministry of children of God, should always be characterized by humility. The Scriptures clearly teaches that God resists the proud, but gives grace to the humble. If therefore, God opposes you because of your proud and arrogant disposition, then I wonder what you can achieve without the grace of God!

Little wonders that in few circumstances, miracles that used to occur when some prayed, now occurs at a decreasing level, or no longer happens at all; and it may also sound weird to learn that some of such fame-seeking, bogus-title "prayer warriors" go out of their way, even to place orders for charms and magic wands from some Indian magicians and elsewhere, just to enable them create pandemonious motions when they prayed, in order to pull crowds! So beware so that no one deceives you, ok? Get to know and experience God personally through His Word and prayer. Ask Him to reveal Himself to you, and He will! One of the sure ways to get deceived, is when you form the habit of running after all manners of miracles instead of seeking and studying to know the truth of the Word of God.

To conclude this chapter, let me point out that the word "repentance" is not only applicable to stark unbelievers. It is indeed applicable to everyone --- believers and those who are yet to believe alike! Chances are 99% out of 100 that someone may be guilty of what we have discussed in the foregoing text. If this assumption is correct, then do not read any further until you have resolved the matter in your spirit. Repent of any error of way you may have found yourself. Tell God you are sorry; then ask Him to forgive you of your proud and bogus approach to issues which may have led you to error. Or possibly you may have been deceived in the past, by running after miracles. If so, tell God you are sorry; then ask the Holy Spirit to help you to turn a new leaf as He might reveal to you or along the lines discussed above. Learn the habit of depending on God moment by moment prayerfully as you face the issues of life. God bless you!

Your prayer life should be a growing experience; and you should not only mature in prayer, at least being able to effectively table your issues before your Heavenly Father by reminding Him of His Word and promises, as opposed to being always prayed for by someone! It is even expected that after some time of being a believer, you should be able to teach others to pray, starting from members of your immediate family, or those you lead to the saving knowledge of Christ; just like our Lord Jesus Christ taught his disciple to pray. Of course, you cannot give what you do not have. In other words, you should always teach from your own practical experiences and by example. So a Covenant person must be a person of prayer in character and practice!

CHAPTER FIVE

THE COVENANT WOMAN

"And God said, Let us make man in our image, after our likeness; and let them have dominion over the fish of the sea, and over the foul of the air, and over the cattle, and over all the earth, and over every creeping thing that creepeth upon the earth. So God created man in his own image; in the image of God created he them. And God blessed them, and God said unto them, Be fruitful and multiply, and replenish the earth and subdue it.." [Gen. 1:26-28] [KJV]

By the time this book is launched, you might either have already celebrated the "Mothers Day" or perhaps looking forward to the next celebration! And you might therefore reason out and say, if Mothers' Day is celebrated, then obviously there should be no doubt that women belong to the covenant heritage! Or you may choose to passively watch out on the outcome of the opinion pool. Well, whichever posture you choose to take, is ok; but you should also be prepared to adjust your posture once you become better informed about the subject matter. So come along with us on this on this memory lane!

From what we now know, it is an incontrovertible fact that the womenfolk do belong to the covenant heritage as we saw in Chapter two of our text. However, for avoidance of doubt, we shall research into this a little further. For best results, the Womenfolk, irrespective of their social status, are supposed to operate under the authority of their husbands when spiritual issues are at stake, for best spiritually beneficial results. If you take a second look at our topical text above [Gen. 1:26-28], you would notice about two language usages that some language students will pick bones with. The first one is in verse 26, where the statement in part, read:

"And God said, Let us make man in our image...." Then the second part says "...and let them have dominion."

Man here was used as a singular noun, but the pronoun referring to man in the second sentence, used a plural pronoun "them." Quite interesting, isn't it? The second unconventional usage is also found in verse 27, where it states:

"So God created man (singular) in his own image;"

The second part says again: "…in the image of God created he him." (Again, a singular pronoun); and then "male and female created he them." (plural).

Then in verse 28, it states as follows: **"And God said unto them: Be fruitful and multiply…."**

So you could see the various use of man, they, him, them, etc. all referring to one person, man! In this text, you would obviously be right to suggest by language standards, that there was no mention of "woman." However, by implication and application, woman is very much in that text, as we shall soon discover.

If we attempt an exploratory look at the story of creation in Genesis, it will be seen that after God created the heaven and the earth, the Scriptures states that the earth was without form and void, dominated only by waters, darkness, and of course the Spirit of God which moved on the face of the waters. Awesome! Then came light to separate darkness, and to represent Day, while darkness represented the night. So evening and morning became the product of the first day. Then the firmament and the division of the waters etc. became the product of the second day.

Then the third day witnessed the gathering together of the waters unto one place to create room for dry land, bringing forth grass, herb-yielding seed, and different kinds of fruit-yielding trees, whose seed is in itself. Then the fourth day witnessed the creation of heavenly bodies that promote the day and the night, signs, seasons, and for days and years.

The sun and moon and the stars were also created on the fourth day. The fifth day also brought about all the sea creatures, the fishes, the whales, the crocodiles, as well as different kinds of fouls of the air, with the command to multiply and fill the seas, and the air. Then the sixth day brought about different living creatures after their kind, cattle, and creeping things, beasts of the earth after their kind (paraphrased).

If these creatures were expected to multiply and fill their different environments, then it implies that "after their kind" used in that Scripture means male and female. Well, we shall allow another Scripture to interpret that context: In Genesis Chapter 7, before the flood, it records as follows:

"The LORD then said to Noah, "Go into the ark, you and your whole family, because I have found you righteous this generation. Take with you, seven of every kind of clean animal, a male and its mate, and two of every kind of unclean animal, male and its mate; and also seven of every kind of bird, male and female, to keep their various kinds alive throughout the earth. (vv.1-3).

So, you could also see that one creature and the opposite sex are implied in the creation account in Genesis. That means right from start, God knew what his blue print was both for the beasts of the field, the creatures of the sea, and of course, for man, who was made in His very image. It is therefore not an accident of nature that God decided to make a complete man in one unit.

By one complete man here, we mean, man and woman put together as one. Don't you ever think that you are more knowledgeable in any way than God; --- Not even on issues of language. On the contrary, any time you see anything that appears unconventional in language, then you should take extra care and time to research further so as to catch the actual meaning of the context. In First Corinthians 1:25, the Scripture says:

"...the foolishness of God is wiser than men; and the weakness of God is stronger than men."

So that's that! It would also be quite reasonable to believe that if God commanded this dual man which He made, to be fruitful, and to multiply and to replenish the earth, then that possibly could have been quite practicable in that their initial dual state of being!

Are we then trying to imply that there is nothing like woman status from the beginning? The answer is "Quite correct!" On the other hand, Scripturally speaking, when you talk of a man, woman should automatically be implied. I believe God our maker, is wiser than anybody. The Scripture even states that *'God's foolishness is wiser than men.'*

Another question that would naturally crop up here is: Are we trying also to imply that a man is not complete without a woman in the picture? That may also be a dual reality!

Well, May God grant us more insights of this text, so that we will really appreciate the type of unity expected in a contemporary marital relationship. Usually when things go wrong, to find a solution, the best thing to do is to go back to Scriptures. Once we get it right, then everything falls into appropriate sequence, because the family concept, is God's original idea, and the Bible, life's manual.

DO YOU THINK THE FEMININE IDEA WAS AN AFTER-THOUGHT?

I wish to submit that the creation of the womenfolk was definitely part and parcel of the original man-package in creation; so there is no question about that. But as to whether giving her a separate physical identity is an after-thought, the answer is a definite "Yes." In case there is an iota of doubt in your mind, I'd suggest you jot it down, while we go on; as I'm sure that such doubts will vanish as we explore the Word further. On a more serious note, I wish to submit here, that once we begin to rediscover the womenfolk, not as a separate entity but rather as a vital component of man, at least within the context of marriage, then we would be getting ready for a vital spiritual and moral revival primarily in the church, and then the nation at large, of which the family is a vital unit. Usually the concept of 1+1=1 which is often revisited during contemporary wedding ceremonies, but forgotten soon afterwards, need not be over-emphasized here [See Gen 2:24].

If indeed, women are vital components of men, then they should equally be filled with a sense of belonging when topics such as this is being addressed -"The Covenant Man In Contemporary Times."

That is to say all the challenges posed to man, equally applies to the womenfolk because before God, all souls are equal!

Before we go further, we should use this opportunity to congratulate all mothers, and wish them well on the occasion of the Mothers' Day celebrations – past, ongoing, or present. Obviously, as the procreation program now stands, once you talk of the Fathers' Day, it is either that the Mothers' Day has already been celebrated, or it is in perspective. In most cases, both parties take pride in each other's celebration because both are God's co-laborers in executing God's extended program for planet earth.

Now, back to our subtopic: After the dual man, Adam has been formed, and assigned to the duty of naming and determining the names to be given to God's lovely creatures, most of these creatures already had their own partners; but in any case, none was a perfect match for Adam in terms of companionship. At best, some of them could be pets to Adam, but definitely not a matching companion! This point is very important and I'd love us to read up a little from Scriptures about this.

It says: **"And Adam gave names to all cattle and to the fowl of the air, and to every beast of the field; but** for Adam, there was not found an help meet for him." [Gen. 2:20].

That means, although he had been formed and mobilized, being male and female in one physical expression, yet he badly needed someone in a separate physical entity; and something had to be done about that by the Omniscient God. There was no indication that Adam made any serious complaint about his loneliness, nor concerning the occupational, or professional hazards inherent in his assignments; so he simply and happily carried out his assigned duties of giving names to God's creatures.

However, God eventually saw the need for a separate physical companion who will also be in the image of a man, though with a womb.

So he proceeded to extract the feminine Adam from the man Adam. Thus the physical presence of the feminine Adam, (woman) was indeed like the Creator's afterthought, but at the same time, aimed at enhancing the performance of the Man- Adam. So, while the women folk today, serve as co-laborers with men, in bringing humanity to birth on planet earth, it is also noteworthy that the first woman in the person of Eve, was delivered from a Man!

THE FIRST SURGICAL OPERATION PERFORMED:

Now, after God decided on what to do to provide his beloved Adam a helpmate, the date was set; and the Scripture records that:

"...the Lord God caused a deep sleep to fall upon Adam...and he took one of his ribs, and closed up the flesh instead thereof. And the rib which the Lord God had taken from man, made he a woman, and brought her unto the man. And Adam said this now is bone of my bones, and flesh of my flesh; she shall be called woman, because she was taken out of man." [Gen. 2:21-23].

I do get quite excited a lot when I read my Bible and discover where the origin of most works of arts, science, architecture,

medicine, and even public administration originated from! Suffice to say from the birth of the physical Eve, we could see how God performed the first major surgical operation! First he applied a deep sleep syndrome, which today, is called anesthetics in medical circles, causing Adam to fall into a deep sleep prior to the operation.

From there, he proceeded to extract some vital organs, and to close the opening with flesh.

Some folks are in the habit of criticizing education by saying "...You don't need education to serve God...etc." Well, that's their own opinion; and I wish them well in their reasoning! However, I think the ideal thing to do, is to encourage all manner of education, provided such is seen as a rediscovery effort of what God has already put in place! To me, education in the hands of an unbeliever, can easily be abused and idolized! But to a believer, it is simply a research and rediscovery effort of what our God has already put in place. Well, this is not too relevant to the topic on hand. We shall give more attention to this issue in subsequent chapters.

A MISSING CUATIONARY CODE FOR MOTHER EVE:

As we have seen so far, it is true to say that God meant well for the Man-Adam by bringing the physical Eve into being. But one may question and say, If indeed God meant well for the Man Adam, being an all-knowing God He is, perhaps it would have been necessary to provide some 'operating instructions' so to speak, concerning the Woman Adam, who now has a physical expression in the person of Mother Eve; at least knowing their inherent possible moral weakness. If you were to suggest, I'm sure at that point in time, you would pen down something like these:

- The Commandments of the Lord God should not be questioned nor altered.

- Behold she is been given to you to fulfill the need for companionship; so do not leave her alone in the house while you are in the field; but always keep a company of each other.

- All issues of decision-making should be taken together.

- Even delegated responsibilities should be scrutinized while being implemented.

- There should be no third-party interference in this relation- ship.

- Any issue of doubt, should be referred to Man-Adam for clarification.

Although these rules may not be exhaustive, but definitely it is felt that some of them would have been necessary and useful, since Woman-Adam who had just arrived, is new in the scene, and therefore, inexperienced in the state of affairs in the garden!

But more importantly, being the All-Knowing God He is, I also feel he must have expected each of them to exercise their will power; and perhaps also leave some lessons to learn for generations to come, on issues of obedience and Godly fear.

Indeed, the will power given to everyone to exercise is what makes each person an individual he or she really is; and not a robot. Of course, it goes without saying that each person will give an account of how this will power was actually exercised here on earth, in the end. You are warned!

All through the Scriptures, the women folks function best as complements to men---helpmates! And that indeed, is their God-given role. Anything to the contrary invariable results in abuse of power! Indeed, if your desire is to live a Godly lifestyle, you should not hesitate to ask yourself the question, "What would God have me do in a situation like this?" Once that is the posture of your heart and mind, then the Spirit of God will always supply you the relevant answers; and eventually you never can go wrong!

Godly women are clothed with the grace to comply most of the time, and not to resist the authority of their husbands, even under pressure---what you may call a compliance spirit; for in so doing, God's grace upon them finds full expression! Often you hear it said like a precept, that 'women are gullible.' It simply suggests that by nature, they are not made to withstand much persuasion, like their men counterparts can. In other respects, they can favorably compete with the men. For instance, the womenfolk are no less intelligent than their men counterparts; neither are they any less imaginative or artistic.

As a matter of fact, given appropriate orientation, contemporary women can function competently in most fields of endeavor like their men counterparts. Of course, if you look around today, you would tell the story yourself. Women are today in virtually every field of endeavor, and even professions that used to be thought to be masculine in nature. For instance, you can find women in the space shuttle team, as pilots, as bus drivers, as train drivers, in different field of engineering, they are in the army; and they want to be ordained as priests; you name it. To crown it all, some of them even excel in these rare fields, as if to affirm the saying that "whatever a man can do, women can equally do!"

So there are very few things that contemporary women can not do by way of skillful adaptation and /or intelligence today. However, there is an extra-emotional grace that they have from God; and this is what distinguishes them as women. This probably explains why serpent the devil, in its subtlety, was able to easily beguile, convince and by implication, deceived Adam's helpmate (Eve) with just a little cross-examination and persuasion over a crucial life and death divine command!

To think about it, Eve must have indeed been so naïve about the whole incident, as to begin to open up her "website" to such a strange creature like a serpent, on an issue she should know much better about, or shall we say, an issue she was not conversant with! May be, because she was just a freshman on the scene! The opinion pool says Mother Eve should have been able to tell this strange visitor off; since in any case, it was merely a talking reptile whom she was not familiar with; or if she wanted to be courteous to this strange visitor, she could have asked him or it, to come back when her husband was around, in case the issue at stake was of such an interest and concern to him (the serpent)! Alternatively, she could have referred the serpent to the originator of the command - God of course, rather than entertaining unfamiliar inquiries that she had little or no accurate answers to!

Another thing that should have aroused her curiosity was the oddities of such a visit, which included the timing, when her husband, the head of the home was not around; then the unfamiliar topic raised by this strange visitor! All these taken together, should have compelled her not to open up her discussion channel at all, to this deceiver!

Apparently, she lacked the spirit of discernment as to know what was at stake in that scenario; and so she took it for a joke. This of course explains why she made a serious mess of the situation.

Today, you still find many strange visitors knocking at your door, (may be, not in the form of a serpent); some of these may even wear some religious appearances. But if you apply your gift of discernment, you discover equally that first of all, the timing is wrong; and probably it coincides with your church time or other important schedules. Secondly, if you dare let such visitors in, you discover that their topics are controversial, and contrary to sound doctrine that you are brought up with; and therefore there is nothing about them you can easily and comfortably accommodate within your time frame for such an unscheduled visit! So every woman should learn a lesson from the experience of Eve and be warned. "To be forewarned is to be forearmed!" goes an old saying. The enemy may still be lurking around today, seeking whom to deceive because his time though short, is not yet over.

Some have also said, if they see the devil coming clearly like a serpent, then they would be more careful! But we need to be even more careful when you do not see the tempter coming like a serpent, because the situation can be more dangerous when the enemy disguises himself like an angel of light! Any time you sense him coming, the prescribed solution is to utter an arrow prayer like a shout of "JESUS" or "BLOOD OF JESUS" etc. In other words, **"submit to God, and then RESIST THE DEVEIL (emphasis mine), and he will flee from you."**

It is indeed better to resist him once you discern his presence, or approach than be messed up by this deceiver. Some would shout "THE BLOOD OF JESUS!" or simply "JESUS!" when they sense a danger signal. Yes, that might be quite helpful, because of its spiritually impactful.

Thus Eve was deluded into believing a lie; and consequently she ate the forbidden fruit thereby crossing the mercy line! Adam too, when he returned from work, took so much for granted! He never asked his wife how she fared in his absence, and whether anybody called for his attention, and stuff like that; neither did Eve bother to narrate her interaction with the strange visitor; but appeared rather more anxious about passing on the forbidden fruit to Adam; and without a question, Adam accepted and ate everything his better-half had presented to him. Some think it was out of overwhelming love for his wife that he did that! Do you think so? It is quite possible!

The bottom line is that he accepted the accursed meal, and ate everything, line, hook and sinker, without asking any question or raising any objections whatsoever. And in so doing, they ended up changing not only their own destiny, but the entire course of God for the human race!

There is a controversial subjective school of thought that 'God knew that Adam and Eve would eat the forbidden fruit, etc., etc., and so made a provision for it! Well, our God is indeed an *All-knowing God!* It is also true that God never made man as a zombie! It is rather true that He made man (and woman) in His own image and likeness. Furthermore, it also true that He gave us Will-Power to exercise. Our knowledge and experience of Scriptures should tell us that everyone will also be accountable for the way we exercise this loaned will-power in the end! I think this is a more objective approach to this issue!

Now back to our where we were, a single mistake you make with an issue of faith can have a far-reaching implication than you can imagine. But the important message here is that before you even eat any meal, you should always look before you leap --- Pray! Another one is that you should desist from the habit of toying with holy things any time, and anywhere!

But thank God for Jesus Christ, the Second Adam; for through Him today, humanity can now come back to relation- ship with God, once you are washed in His Blood of the Covenant. In Him, the Eden lost by the first Adam is today, being restored unto man!

THE WOMAN AS A "WOMB MAN"

Some popular scholars have opined that the name, woman as given by Adam to his helpmate was in deed, short for "womb man;" and some of the reasons adduced are as follows: In addition to possessing a womb, women also possess most of the other attributes that exist in a man, namely, a man has spirit; he has a soul, and he has a body; and the same is true of a woman. Some research has also revealed that Godly women are highly talented and knowledgeable; they are endowed with rare capabilities that men also have; and sometimes, more; yet in most cases, clothed with so much grace, humility and humor, that they would hardly show that they know anything! But wait until by chance, one occasion or another prompts any of them to voice out their feeling or opinion on any issue, then you are shocked concerning the degree of wisdom they possess!

However, while we admit that women are part and parcel of the Covenant heritage, some members of the womenfolk seem to take so much for granted in the adaptation of their primary distinguishing factor, the womb, to God's purpose. Thus, some either deliberately shirk this primary responsibility of the use of the womb, or they take things for granted, and in pretence, aim for certain roles meant for the men folk! You may ask, how can that be? And I'll tell you that some members of the women-folk take it upon themselves overtly or covertly to birth-control the issues they wish to have; worse still, some even decide against having children at all, etc. But whatever our differences are, let's go back to the basics as revealed in the Word of God!

It is important we realize that we do not actually own our own bodies; but God does! And according to Scriptures, a woman has no right over her own body, but her husband does. Therefore, issues concerning how many children to have should not be an issue of unilateral decision of anybody; if anything, it should be a bi-lateral and mutual one---between husband and wife and in the process of reaching that decision, the husband should be the 'chairman,' because he is the head of the home! And in fact, the head of the woman according to Scriptures; and do not forget this: The ultimate aim is to make for a wonderful peaceful, harmonious godly home. Obviously our God is wiser than anybody!

Really, it might not be out of place for a couple to choose the number of children they feel they can comfortably BRING UP FOR GOD (emphasis mine). In some cases, it may be necessary to limit the number of such a choice, due to certain critical reasons which may be socio-economic, or health reasons. But where all things are equal, and there is no health concerns, then couples should, under God, yield themselves to God's divine purpose thereby contributing their quota to fill their immediate environment with as many Godly children as possible! Thanks to couples who have their '...*quiver full of them!* If it is Scriptural, then it must be expedient!

Finally, note that this topic is being discussed with every sense of responsibility, since the author is also blessed with a godly mom, sisters, a wife and a daughter. So to cap it up, let every couple owe it as a responsibility to God, to bring to birth, at least two children (one boy and one girl) into the world; and more importantly to bring them up in fear and nurture of the Lord! It is never enough to just give birth to them and abandon them; rather the job is more complete when children are also brought up in the fear and nurture of God!

It is also true that there are some who seek to have children, but this hope is delayed. The Bible indeed says it all: *"Hope delayed makes the hearth sick......"* (Proverbs 13, verse 12). If you are there, then I have a good news for you: Our God can meet that particular need of yours right now, if you have faith and believe that He CAN; because His Promises are *"yea and amen."* Neither will He change His Word because of your situation. You see, oftentimes, we, humans are the problem because we prefer to take the "doctor's report" or the opinions of people around you, rather than that of God. Much as it is easier for some to have issues (children) with little or no effort, yet if you are a child of God and have difficulty in this area, bear in mind that God is never limited by time, space, circumstance or situation to a person who believes in Him, and by faith comes to Him with any need. Once you could develop this FAITH mind-set, then nothing will be impossible for you. The second part of the above Scripture says: *"....but when the desire cometh...it is a tree of life."*

You should note that your success, or prosperity, or progress only glorifies God! In fact, such achievements give Him considerable pleasure! So if you would pray along the foregoing lines, be sure that God will grant you the desires of your heart. So stop whatever you're doing right now, and pour out your heart to God in prayer. Do it right now! The verse of Scripture that follows is also important: It says: "Whose despises the Word shall be destroyed; but he that *feareth* the commandment shall be rewarded. (Prov. 13:13). I do not know how serious you take the Word of God? I pray to see all that change right now, in your own interest ok? Bless you!

Another issue, and perhaps a new spiritual paradigm concerning child-bearing is the issue of possession. Who do you think owns the children you bring up? And who gives the ability to bear these children anyway? The obvious answer to the two questions is of course, "Our Heavenly Father!"

If you agree that this is the right answer, then can you tell me why you would choose to have a plan that is antithetical to God's repopulation program, knowing fully well that the fruits of the womb that result from marital union are ultimately God's property; and you, only a vessel of honor, and perhaps a caretaker!

You see, as rational beings, the time has come when we should rationalize things properly in accordance with the Word of God, and all the principles of the New Kingdom to which we now belong --- the Kingdom of God of course! Some of us take certain measures that we cannot justify; yet the Scripture has told us that:

"**....the time of ignorance, God overlooks.**" If our God overlooks the time of ignorance, which should now be in the past for the average believer, then why should we still be living and doing things in ignorance?

So let's stop putting restraints to our partnership with God; even in issues of bearing Godly seeds, because His command remains that we should "**...multiply and replenish the earth...**" Yes! And I'm sure if we do that, our Heavenly Father will be well pleased for such a gesture. I believe, nothing can be better than doing things that will give God much pleasure! This issue should not be controversial at all, to those know the truth! And I'm sure you do!

Today, the irony is that the phenomenon of population explosion is associated with the developing countries as opposed to industrialized countries.

Oftentimes, you hear people criticize the economic topic of job outsourcing to developing countries. Some do that without knowing the details of what is involved. The simple reason for jobs-outsourcing is of course, demographic factors! Where there is population explosion, many of God's resources are brought down within easy reach. Thus there will be availability of cheap labor supply, both for the Lord's vineyard, and for socio-economic purposes. Secondly, in times of war, there will be abundant supply of able-bodied men and women to enlist in the armed forces and help defend our nation's territorial integrity; and of course, to man various sophisticated machinery. Thirdly, God's earth is adequately occupied without leaving a vacuum as He originally intended! Also, a large population easily generates greater resources which make for smooth running of governance.

As records has it, however, the under population scenario in industrialized states can be attributable to a deliberate and strict birth-control measures adopted by couples of child-bearing age (which gesture, may not be holistically justifiable). You also have modernity-associated abortions as another factor. So, you can imagine why there have been so many debates on abortion legalization in contemporary times. As you know, the devil would always question or try to compromise any standard set by God! We also know that some abortionist gestures result from irresponsible and irrational desires of some ungodly folks to indulge in pre-marital, or extra-marital sex, while at the same time, trying to avoid the responsibilities that go with it! (Child-bearing and upbringing of course!) Others, for reasons best known to them, simply go all out to raise children outside of wedlock! If this describes you, then it is time you stopped toying with holy things! So hear what the Word of God says to you here:

"...In the past, God overlooked such ignorance; but he commands all people everywhere to repent...." [Acts 17:30] NIV.

Yes, repentance is actually a spiritual exercise for everyone: believers and potential believers alike; and it is simply an act of turning away from any presumptuous habit(s) (big or small) which go against the will of God. So, what you have to do, DO QUICK!

However, most women these days seem to be much more informed on issues of life and godliness, such that they operate at very high spiritual frequency! No wonder, many women are finding their ways into the priestly functions today, as Pastors; though a few churches still keep the doors closed to the quest for women ordination. It is true that by nature, the womenfolk are quite gullible, and yield easily to temptations; yet, a handful of the womenfolk are quite spiritually-determined, especially those of them who minister with the support and approval of their husbands.

While it is true that certain fundamental issues is always there, as revealed by Scriptures, yet spirit-filled believers should not discriminate against the womenfolk; after all, those of them who were members of the early church, played very important and useful roles; and of course, the Holy Ghost fell upon them all equally at Pentecost without discrimination. Prominent amongst them were Mary the mother of John, Tabitha also known as Dorcas, who was described as a woman full of good works (see Acts 9:36-41); Mary the sister of Lazarus, whom Jesus raised from the dead (Luke 10:38), to name but a few. In the light of these, the womenfolk should be warmly welcomed, given equal opportunity to serve God as they feel led, realizing that they are co-heirs of the Promise, according to Scriptures. That means giving a second rate treatment to the womenfolk in the service of God is disobeying the Scriptures; and men are the worse offenders in this regard! For instance, in certain cultures, a man is allowed to take as many women as he can manage, as wives; and in so doing several human rights and socio-economic issues are negatively compromised.

Also, it is noteworthy that until 1922 in most parts of the U.S, women were not allowed to vote or be voted for; in other words, they were disenfranchised (using a political science language). In other parts of the world: Africa, Asia, Latin America and the Middle East, women are generally not allowed to express their opinion openly and freely. Yet we know that there are certain socio-economic and political issues where it is ideal that women be represented by their kind, because they know issues that affect them better! Thus the representation of the womenfolk in government circles, is still a novelty in those places.

Now let's see the Bible's perspective about the womenfolk. It says:

"Likewise ye husbands, dwell with them according to knowledge, giving honor unto the wife, as unto the weaker vessel, and as being heirs together of the grace of life; that your prayers be not hindered." [1Peter 3:7].

It is that serious! That means if you want your prayers to achieve their desired goal, which is getting the attention of God, with happy returns, then you should not despise your wife. Also, in Colossians 3:19, the Bible also says:

"Husbands, love your wives, and be not bitter against them."

You may say, after all, this is talking about the home scenario. Then let's take a look at 1Tim. 5:1-2: It says

> *"Rebuke not an elder; but intreat the elder women as mothers; the younger as sisters, with all purity."*

So it is important that we accord each one their respective places in the scheme of things. Finally on this, let's also see what the Scriptures say in 1Cor. 6:9. It goes on to say,

> *"Know yet not that the unrighteous shall not inherit the Kingdom of God?"* And it went on to itemize them, for avoidance of doubt: *"Be not deceived, neither fornicators, nor idolaters, nor adulterers, nor effeminate, nor abusers of themselves with mankind, nor thieves, nor covetous, nor drunkards, nor revilers, nor extortioners, shall inherit the Kingdom of God."*

All these acts of ungodliness are categorized here as equal; that means if you contravene the law of God in any of these ways, you are hereby warned! No sitting on the fence on this issue---It is either you are in, or you are out; or you are either hot, or you are cold. If in deed, you are not observing and obeying the Word of God towards godliness then you are going the opposite direction and by so doing, knowingly or unknowingly diverting yourself from the Kingdom of God.

Whatever your situation is however, there is good news for you: You still have this perhaps last chance to make a "U" turn to God by simply confessing your sins to God, and accepting Jesus Christ into your life, as your Lord and Savior. Do it now!

Finally, much as you could say the creation of the womenfolk may be an afterthought thing, but from the foregoing text, you could also see that they are definitely part and parcel of men; and by implication, that could mean that one may be incomplete without the other! In other words, a man is yet incomplete without a woman! Or more appropriately, a woman is made within the context of a man. And this gets full expression as soon as a man finds his 'missing rib' or in other words, a wife!

Let me try to conclude this chapter with an *adapted* literary work, titled *"God's Letter to A Woman."* Of course, you should know that *"...the woman"* here refers to all the womenfolk! You could see from this inspired poetry that your roles are very unique in the scheme of things! Indeed, if the program of God to populate the earth were to be possible, then the role of the women folk is simply indispensable! Now, read on!

Another cross-section of Women's Day Celebrations at the African Christian Fellowship, in Houston, Texas.(4)

GOD'S LETTER TO A WOMAN
"My dear daughter:

When I created the heavens and the earth, I spoke them into being

When I created man, I formed him and breathed life into his nostrils.

But you, woman, I fashioned after I breathed the breath of life into man, because your nostrils are too delicate.

I allowed a deep sleep so that he could not interfere with the creativity.

From one bone, I fashioned you. I chose the bone that protects man's life.

I chose the rib, which protects his heart and lungs and supports him, as you are meant to do. Around this one bone, I shaped you....I modeled you. I created you perfectly and beautifully.

Your characteristics are as the rib; strong yet delicate and fragile.

You provide protection for the most delicate organ in man, his heart.

His heart is the center of his being; his lungs hold the breath of life.

The ribcage will allow itself to be broken before it will allow damage to the heart.

Support man as the rib cage supports the body. You were not taken from his feet, to be under him, nor were you taken from his head, to be above him. You were taken from his side, to stand beside him and be held close to his side.

You are my perfect angel! You are my beautiful little girl.

You have grown to be splendid women of excellence, and my eyes fill when I see the virtues in your heart. Your eyes...don't change them. Your lips, how lovely when they part in prayer. Your nose, so perfect to form.

Your hands so gentle to touch. I've caressed your face in your deepest sleep.

I've held your heart close to mine. Of all that lives and breathes, you are most like me.

Adam walked with me in the cool of the day, yet he was lonely. He could not see me or touch me. He could only feel me.

So everything I wanted Adam to share and experience with me, I fashioned in you; my Holiness, my Strength, my Purity, my Love, my Protection and Support.

You are special because you are an extension of me. Man represents my image, woman my emotions. Together, you represent the totality of God.

So man.....treat woman well. Love her, respect her, for she is fragile. In hurting her, you hurt Me. What you do to her, you do to Me. In crushing her, you only damage your own heart; the heart of your Father, and the heart of her Father.

Women, support man. In humility, Show him the power of emotion I have given you.

In gentle quietness, show him the power of emotion I have given you.

In gentle quietness, show your strength.

In love, show him that you are the rib that protects his inner self.

Did you not know that woman is special in God's eyes?

Remember, "God does not give you any task without giving you the tools to get it done!" Bless you!"

Author's Note: Give a (godly) woman her place in the home, then you bring out the best in a man!

REVIEW:

- Under what circumstance should a man or woman stay alone?
  Discuss.

- In the light of Adam and Eve in the Garden of Eden before the fall, do you think that God expects man to have a fore taste of heaven while yet on earth? Back up your response with Scripture.

- What is the middle point in an ideal marital relationship? Discuss.

- Then do we actually have covenant women on their own merit?

- If your answer to (4) is negative, then are there any exceptions to the rule?

CHAPTER SIX

The Covenant Man As A Family Man

Here is a trustworthy saying: If anyone sets his heart on being an overseer (bishop), he desires a noble task. Now the overseer must be above reproach, the husband of one wife, temperate, self-controlled, respectable, hospitable, able to teach, not given to drunkenness, not violent, but gentle, not quarrelsome, not a lover of money. He must manage his own family well and see that his children obey him with proper respect. If anyone does not know how to manage his own family, how can he take care of God's church?

(1Tim. 3:1-5)NIV.

Absolutely true! The Covenant man should be a family man!! In one of the Scriptures about Covenant man Abraham, God made a very important pronouncement about him, in Gen. 18, saying:

For I know him that he will command his children and his household after him, and they shall keep the way of the LORD, to do justice and judgment, that the LORD may bring upon Abraham, that which he hath spoken of him.(verse 19).

Obviously, the Lord is an all-knowing God; but we as humans are often guided by what the eyes can see, or manifest evidences. So, if we were to assess Abraham's family management capability and inclinations based on his handling of the affairs of his immediate family, we could see that he loved his wife, even though their children were late in coming into the picture; after all, he knew that children were in God's hands to give; and that He that called him out of his kindred, was equally able to supply all his needs according to His riches in glory, as it were, and that there was nothing whatsoever too difficult for him to do, etc. etc.

Now, I wish to pause and ask this question: "What is your own estimation of God?" Everyone indeed, should be able to define God in his or her own terms, based on their intrinsic experiences with Him. As for Abraham, he was totally consumed by his idea of God as the ALMIGHTY!!! This could be seen in Abraham's absolute posture in his responses whenever God called his attention to a thing.

Needless state that if you have an ordinary level idea about God, your experience of Him cannot go beyond that level! I would urge you therefore, to begin to develop a large heart about God. Think of Him as Who He really is: the Almighty Creator of heaven and earth, the seas and the mountains all that are in them. Think of Him as Most Merciful Father! Think of Him as our Savior and Deliverer Who in His mercy, worked out another restoration program for the fallen man, which culminated in sacrificing His only begotten son, Jesus Christ on the Calvary Cross, to restore man to Himself. I mean, you should have a better idea of God now even more than some saints of old did! Or at least better than those who are yet outside the Covenant! So change your perspective of God today, and stop limiting Him. Once you do this, then you will begin to see your whole life assume a new and different dimension for the better.

Now back to Abraham as a family man: Let us now extend his relationship to Lot, his cousin, who accompanied him on his expedition with God (so to speak!) Before that, let me also observe that his love for his wife was not a one-sided affair; the wife also reciprocated through submission. The Scripture tells us that Sarah called her husband, "Lord!" And for a lady to call her husband Lord, it portrays a sense of total submission to the man's authority.

Now, on his relationship with Lot, his cousin, it would appear that Lot received the treatment of a first son! All of a sudden, we saw that Lot started to have his own flocks, almost immediately that he came to the scene; and there was no record of his passing through a period of apprenticeship or servitude like the case with Jacob and his uncle, Laban.

Lot became wealthy in the house of his wealthy uncle, so much so that according to Scriptures, the land was not able to accommodate his men and those of his uncle's as well as their numerically multiplying cattle.

For purposes of emphasis, let us see how the Scriptures records Abraham's reaction. It states as follows:

"Abram said unto Lot: Let there be no strife, I pray thee, between me and thee, and between my herdsmen and thy herdsmen, for we be brethren."

Think of that! The degree of provocation was so high; but even at that, Covenant man Abraham did not show it; rather, he took it all calmly or probably, prayerfully. He did not start recalling Lot's poor parental background, nor about how he had accommodated and fed him over the years until now! I mean it would have been logical for him to dress Lot down based on his unmannerly, inordinate ambition, as well as his manifestation of immature youthful exuberance; but he never did that!

Apparently Abraham did not want any distractions from his focus on God, his Maker and Benefactor.

Now let me pause here to ask a pertinent question: How do you react to issues concerning your children, your wife, and perhaps issues affecting your siblings and other distant relations? Do you realize that it is a responsibility you have to manage those affairs and to bring about peace in the whole scenario? It can be nauseating to find some men who sound so religious, but are terribly mean to their household, resulting in apparent lack of peace and order in the home! If this describes you, then you should go back and get things right, right now! If you do not do that, you will make no good success of your religious pursuits; because, as far as our God is concerned, it is 'Peace at home first!' period!

The Scriptures says:

"Blessed are the peace makers for they shall be called the sons of God." Matt. 5:19 (paraphrased). But remember, the opposite of this coin is also true; so decide which one you really represent!

The opposite situation is also true, because the Word of God is a two-edged sword! That is to say, if you should toe the line of Abraham by making peace at home, you have peace with God; but if you fail to do so, may be because you are under spouse, self, or peer pressure or whatever pressure as opposed to God-pressure (the fear of the Lord), then the negative would invariably apply!

So the reverse of that Scripture would then be as follows: "Cursed are the trouble makers, for they shall be called the sons of the devil!" But that should not be your portion in Jesus Name. *(Say a loud Amen, if you would.)*

Then, another opportunity of testing came by, and still, Abraham beat it hands down! This time, it was when Lot and his men were due to separate from his uncle. Ideally, when it comes to priority, Abraham's right to be the first to choose between him and his cousin should not be controvertible at all, since obviously, he is the head of household, and the eldest of the two, etc. Yet, probably knowing that this guy, Lot was a greedy type, he decided to concede that option of first choice to him; and as you could see here, without any hesitation or reservation Lot proceeded to take the first choice option!

Let's see the Scriptures again here. It says, Abraham said to Lot:

"Is not the whole land before thee? Separate thyself, I pray thee, from me; if thou will take the left hand, then I will go to the right; or if thou depart to the right hand, then I will go to the left." (Verse 9).

Here, one would have expected Lot to respond discreetly by returning his uncle's rightful place to him; but instead, he ambitiously dabbled into the business of choosing head-long! By his apparent inordinate ambitious approach to things, little wonder that he eventually ended up in the land of the ungodly ---Sodom and Gomorrah of course! From a cursory assessment of Lot's posture here, he seems to be the type that are governed by what the eyes can see, but lack the essential godly character of humility, courtesy and in deed, any sense of decency whatsoever! See how the Scriptures put it:

"And Lot lifted up his eyes and beheld all the plain of Jordan, that it was well watered everywhere, before the Lord destroyed Sodom and Gomorrah....then Lot chose him all the plain of Jordan; and Lot journeyed east and they separated themselves, the one from the other." (verse 11).

By giving up all his rights to this inexperienced greedy boy, one might try to scold Abraham as being too care-free!

Yes, sometimes it is even better to be a fool for Christ's sake. However, this is a case of a Covenant man, who by his experience in walking with his God has no time for any distractions whatsoever! When you walk closely with God, you will easily overcome contemporary trials and temptations. However, suffice to say that by giving up all his rights, he spared himself of the anguish and embarrassments of a greedy, ungrateful Youngman! It was as if Abraham was saying "Take the whole world, and leave me with Jesus! [Peace].

Now, wait a minute! After Lot made his hasty choice of 'the best' of the land based on "*by sight*" standards, it is interesting to hear what happened next: God instantly spoke up! Listen to what He said to Abraham:

"And the Lord said unto Abram, after that Lot was separated from him, Lift up now thine eyes, and look from the

Place where thou art, northward and southward, and east- ward and westward. For all the land which thou seest, to thee will I give it, and to thy seed forever. And I will make thy seed as the dust of earth...." [vv.14-16]KJV.

Yes, the degree of comfort a Covenant man experiences when God speaks a word of comfort in his affliction can be priceless!

However, despite Lot's vulgar behavior towards his uncle during his stay with him, yet it is incredible to observe that Abraham never relented in his efforts to see to Lot's welfare, even at Sodom and Gomorrah, where he got entrapped into as a result of his own error. Thus Abraham left an exemplary mania in accommodating all the inconsistencies of relationship within his immediate family; especially between him and his cousin Lot, despite Lot's outrageous and unbecoming attitudes. From this little sample of his relationship with his immediate family members, we can rightly conclude that he was indeed, an accomplished family man!

Traced back to the creation of Adam, the family has been a unique institution of God's idea; and so he expects all expressions of *charity* to begin there as it were. That means, from Genesis to Revelation, you could trace God's blue print for the family .Our lead text for this chapter speaks volumes of what is expected of any Covenant men of God, as far as his nuclear family is concerned. Once you can grapple with the responsibility of taking care of your immediate family, then you have formed the basis for building a chain of spiritual families; from the known to the unknown! By a spiritual family here, we mean converts: those who come to the saving knowledge of Jesus Christ through your contact with them.

It goes without saying that these ones need a lot of care and nurture. Don't you lead someone to Christ, and abandon such a person to himself, without once in a while, asking him or her, *"How are you doing?* If you do that, you would be like an irresponsible and non-caring parent. Instead, you should continue to relate with your converts like parent-child relationship, until one day, such a person can stand on his own feet spiritually. However, once you lead someone to Christ, your duty should be to pray as if all depends on prayer, and also work as if all depends on that. So in your prayer, try to uphold your convert before God; and in fact literally hand him over to God to protect and keep. And if by reason of proximity your convert is within easy reach, then you do have an extra responsibility to care for him like a spiritual parent too. Even if he or she is far away, you can maintain touch through correspondence and prayer!

In expecting Covenant men to be family men, it is apparent that God does not want anyone to feel that once you are saved, then that is it! Never!! Instead, it should portray a sense of "Saved to Serve" mentality. That means you should continue to re-channel the resources God places in your hands or at your disposal, to productive purposes---to raise more men and women ultimately for the Lord's vineyard!

You might ask, what about those who do not believe in marriage. Well, the answer would simply be that there are indeed those whom the Scripture describes as *eunuchs for the kingdom*. These are the only exception to the rule in raising physical family for the average healthy individual. We may take a look at Scriptures here: It says:

"For there are some eunuchs, which are so born from their mother's womb: and there are some eunuchs, which were made eunuchs of men; and there be eunuchs which have made themselves eunuchs for the kingdom of heaven's sake." [Matt. 19:12].

A recently celebrated eunuch for the kingdom was the late Pope John Paul the second of blessed memory. (May his soul rest in peace!) But then, you cannot say that he was not a family man. As a matter of fact, record has it that he made a tremendous positive impact on the lives of men and women all over the globe even outside the confines of his religious entity. Indeed, the issue of many wanting to become eunuchs for the kingdom has been terribly abused in contemporary times. Many there are, who elect to be eunuchs for the Service of God, and unfortunately, after undergoing all the rituals, and theocratic oaths to be faithful to their *psudo* call to service, only to end up compromising with the oath they voluntarily took, and went back to numerous worldly pursuits!

Thus invariably you find such "ordained" men getting involved in sexual abuses of one kind or the other, including going gay! This is sad and unfortunate! A note of warning here, is that once you are convinced that you are called to the priestly office that requires the oath to celibacy and a holy and godly living, then you should go ahead and take it. Thereafter, prayerfully under the pain of death, you should abide by the terms of your oath, to the glory of God, and your sanctification.

Some people get involved in certain vocations due to one contemporary attraction or the other, or perhaps some other unknown ulterior motives other than the call of God; but incidentally, these are the ones that fall by the way side! History has shown that those who responded to the genuine call of God for their lives, go to any length to keep to the demands of such call to service. However, the truth of the matter is that you don't necessarily need to be a eunuch before you can serve God; more-so, when you do not have a specific call! A lot of service options do abound in God's vineyard with regard to ministerial service in the Lord's vineyard. Let's go back to Scriptures here: It says:

"Flee fornication. Every sin that a man doeth is without the body; but he that committeth fornication sinneth against his own body. What? Know ye not that your body is the temple of the Holy Ghost which is in you, which ye have of God, and ye are not your own? For ye are bought with a price; therefore glorify God in your body and in your spirit, which are God's." [1Cor. 7:18-20].(KJV).

As we have read here, the issue of what you do in your body is not something that is optional to you because you do not really own yourself; rather, you are Somebody's property. You are God's property! Therefore, if you compromise the terms of the Covenant upon your life, you are simply threading off on your eternal destiny with temporal fleeting pleasures of sin; especially, if you call yourself a prophet or a priest of God! No one has ever eaten his or her cake, and still finds it intact in their hands! Never!

However, the good news here is that you can enjoy the privilege of a second chance through the act of repentance and being born again, while there is still time. But when you do repent, do not dare go back to the old road that was impossible for you to thread before, ok? That is to say, do not go back to wear the hood of celibacy anymore because that would amount to carrying a burden you cannot bear successfully. Instead, take a good time out to study the Scriptures so as to get the full context of how to serve God successfully without bearing a yoke you cannot bear; especially when you do not have the call as a kingdom eunuch. In Saint Paul's first letter to the Corinthians, similar issues arose which are quite relevant here. Let's see how those issues were addressed. It says,

"It is good for a man not to touch a woman. Nevertheless, to avoid fornication, let every man have his own wife, and let every woman have her own husband.....Defraud ye not, one the other, except it be with consent for a time , that ye may give yourselves to fasting and prayer; and come together again, that Satan tempt you not for your incontinence."

I have gone this far on this issue, so that we know for sure that Paul here was actually addressing people who pray and fast. That means he was definitely addressing believers in the Lord Jesus Christ --- Covenant men you may say, who found themselves in similar real life situations.

Actually the Scriptures say a lot of positive things concerning two heads as opposed to one! In Ecclesiastes 4, the Bible says as follows:

"Two are better than one, because they have a good reward for their labor. For if they fall, the one will lift up his fellow; but woe to him that is alone when he falls; for he hath not another to help him up. Again, if two lie together, then they have heat; but how can one be warm alone? And if one prevail against him, two shall withstand him; and a three-fold cord is not quickly broken." [Vv. 9-12].

If you can be married and serve God more acceptably, and successfully; and by "successfully" I mean maintaining a clear conscience before God and man; and by not living a life of hypocrisy! And being in good hands with the LORD, and a sure candidate for heaven! If you can achieve that on a daily basis, to me, that is the greatest success anyone can have in all of life's endeavors.

But anyone who thinks that he can succeed in playing hide and seek game, should realize that no one can hide anything from the All-Seeing Eyes of the Almighty God; because, eventually whatever is hidden shall be made manifest; in accordance with Scriptures! Therefore, if you discover that you have signed up for something you cannot sustain, the best thing to do is to make a "U" turn, and begin life all over again rather than risk going to the habitation of the devil and his angels in the end --- hell fire of course! Many known former priests after the order of celibacy have taken this step and today, most of them testify that they are happier for it. Why not you? Make no mistake about it, a life of hypocrisy applies to all kinds of sinful living; so do not think that this passage applies only to ordained priests of any particular denomination, ok? If anything, it is meant for anyone who has not yet secured his or her passport to heaven! And more importantly, pointing you to the WAY --- Jesus Christ, the Savior of the whole world!

On the issue of holiness, one thing is certain: You can succeed in deceiving men, but not God! As indicated earlier Pope John Paul II (of blessed memory) is reckoned as the most successful contemporary kingdom eunuchs known worldwide; there might be a few others in the priestly vocation that are known or unknown to us. It pays to be faithful to God in whatever vocation you choose to occupy.

To counter balance this equation however, I would also mention to you numerous contemporary men of God (Covenant men), who believe that full time priests could get married. However, for want of space and time, I shall decline to mention names in this current edition. Be that as it may, the point being made here is quite clear that God does not impose any undue restraint upon anyone whose heart's desire is to serve Him, and/or live for Him. However, if you take an oath to celibacy or in other words, if you choose to become a eunuch for the kingdom, please try not to breach, or abuse the oath in any way because your life destiny could be tied to it. Remember, God respects oaths, covenants, agreements, etc. It could be a marital oath, a financial agreement, or a priestly oath. If you wish to live for God, and/or to serve Him, it is important that you are mindful of what His likes and dislikes; and as a child of God, behave like a child of your heavenly Father! You could learn more about this by studying His Word, the Bible. In that sense, I'd suggest you try and secure a favorite version, and start studying it in earnest today! It is no surprise therefore, that this whole book has been conceptualized using the life-transforming Biblical philosophy. I'd like to know, if by chance, this edition is of any blessing to you in particular!

To cap it up this chapter, how has the foregoing chapter challenged you? One obvious answer is: If Christ has set you free, you should know it, and then begin now to take advantage of all the New Creation realities open to children of God. In Scriptures, the Lord Jesus Christ says something very relevant here: He says as follows:

"Come to me, all you who are weary and burdened, and I will give you rest. Take my yoke upon you, and learn of me, for I am gentle and humble in heart, and you will find rest for your souls. For my yoke is easy and my burden is light." [Matt. 11:28-30] NIV.

In my humble opinion, except on cases of extreme conviction, it would make no sense to go on to assume a burden that is already borne, and dropped down on your behalf. Christ our Redeemer has already borne all the extraneous religious burdens on our behalf, so that we should not be duplicating efforts by trying to bear them again. If anything, He wants us to begin to labor within the victory that He has already won for us! What we should now do is to allow His Spirit to open our eyes to other areas that deserve urgent attention in our lives, as well as those of other men and women, and to expend any reserve energies upon them, in the Power of the Holy Spirit, by way of contending for the faith prayerfully and through other practical ways! So, as always, your watchword should be "Watch and Pray" or the other way round, "Pray and Work." Some colleagues suggest that 'You pray, as if all depends on prayer; and also to work, as if all depends upon work!"

Perhaps this scenario should give some clue as to why so many presumptuous eunuchs have failed woefully in upholding the demands of their vows. Some for want of what else to do, have opted for same-sex marriage, which Scriptures tell us is an abomination before the Lord. The Scriptures of course warns us that those who practice same-sex marriage will not inherit the kingdom of God, among others. (See 1Cor. 6:9).

In case your Bible is not handy, read it here:

"Do you not know that the wicked will not inherit the kingdom of God? Do not be deceived: Neither the sexually immoral, nor idolater, nor adulterers, nor male prostitutes, nor homosexual offenders...." (NIV).

As we conclude this chapter therefore, please make up your mind right now to know the will of God concerning your life; once you know it, commit your whole self to it, (spirit, soul and body). Our Loving God is the author and originator of the concept of marriage and family life; and nothing can be further from the truth. So, make up your mind to say "Yes" to God on this issue of family, and be a true family covenant man in every Godly sense, in Jesus Name.

Review:

1. Some feel that getting married will make them less commit- ted to God's work, and perhaps less holy. Do you agree with this concept? Discuss, and back up your standpoint with relevant Scriptures and/or testimonies.

- What place would you give homosexuals and all those who abuse sexuality in a contemporary church setting today; and why?

- In what context do you believe that all sins carry equal consequences? Or do you think some sins are more grievous than others?
  Discuss.

CHAPTER SEVEN

Quit You Like Men!

Be thou strong therefore, and shew thyself a man. And keep the charge of the LORD thy God, to walk in his ways to keep his Statutes, and his commandments, and his judgments and his testimonies, as it is written in the Law of Moses, that thou mayest prosper in all that thou doest, and whithersoever thou turnest thyself. [1Kings 2:1-3] KJV.

The above Scriptures were the words of King David (the man the Scriptures refers to as the man after God's heart), to his son, Solomon, his heir designate.

I was extremely touched by the parting words from the heart of a dying man of God, to his beloved son, his heir-designate! And I believe this advice to Solomon is also addressed to you and me----particularly if you are not opportuned to be of a reasonable age when you lost your dad! Then you should take in the entire exhortation as a whole, and personalize it. Definitely, this Scripture does have a far-reaching significance to every man child and I therefore recommended it for everyone's meditation upon!

Now, what is the implication of this Scripture to a Covenant man of our text? Well, if you look closely enough, you would discover that this Scriptural passage is identical to God's charge to Joshua, as he was about to step into the shoes of Moses the Servant of the Lord! Very often, you find the unchanging Word of God repeating itself in similar circumstances and situations. However, in this particular application to Solomon, David said among other things, **"Be thou strong therefore, and shew thyself a man!"** What does this speak to you, the Covenant man in contemporary times?

Above: A Session of Bible Search by some scholars

It is common knowledge that in contemporary times, some men have taken it upon themselves to launch attacks on humanity in the erroneous belief that they are demonstrating religious zeal!

For instance, it is a religious zeal that leads some brainwashed young men, to yield their bodies to be burned, as suicide bombers! In a recent interview with a volunteer suicide bomber, conducted by Time magazine, the guy was saying a lot of funny nonsense as the reason why he chose to enlist as a suicide bomber. Among what he said, was that by his belief in Islam, those who kill go to heaven! When asked how his Allah would view the innocent people they kill in their suicide operation, he answered as follows: "I pray no innocent people are killed in my mission,… But if some are, he went on, I know when they arrive in heaven, Allah will ask them to forgive me."

Can you imagine that level of nonsensical self-delusion? This is definitely a deceit from the pit of hell! The question such guys do not ask themselves is this: If indeed, they are justified in their brainwashed concept, why is it that their leaders and commanders do not dare first set examples by converting their own bodies as human bombs? Why is it only the vagabonds, the *"almajiris"* amongst them that are brainwashed to carry out suicide bombing? And to cap it all up, they are made to believe an error, that after taking their own lives, (which in itself is a capital sin before God); and not only that, after committing large scale murder of innocent people, that they will eventually, still go to heaven! Probably their kind of heaven must be different from the heaven every saint of God aspires to go to! Well, as far as we know, the father of murderers is the king of hell himself: Satan the devil of course; so there is no doubt as to where those who commit atrocities end up! Sad enough, the answer is Hell Fire!

As it were, humanity remains the centerpiece of God's best intentions on Planet Earth; therefore anyone whose activity is destructive of the human race, should in no way, associate such activities with God. It could probably be nothing but merely a religious practice!

Obviously both those who inspire young people to commit such a heinous crimes against humanity, and those who yield themselves to such deception, show that they have lost faith in the human race, and so, are just there to fulfill the blue print of Satan the devil, whose mission is to kill, steal, and to destroy, according to Scriptures (See John 10:10)..

No one reading this pro-life hand book is expected to ever be associated with suicide bombing, or any act that results in shedding innocent blood. So in case the contrary becomes the case, and by divine arrangement this book falls into your hands, I urge you to stop being deceived! Be wise, and smart about your life ok? Stop being deceived because what you are initiated into, will definitely end you up in a place you may not like to go --- hell fire! On a more serious note: Everyone who has attained the age of accountability, shall give an account to God for the way you spent your life here on earth. So don't let anyone deceive you concerning such critical issues of life, k?

You see, it is a good thing to aspire to get to heaven any way! Indeed, heaven is the final home of everyone who has been born again through Jesus Christ, God's provision as Passport to heaven; but you don't get there by taking your own life; not to talk of destroying other innocent people's lives who of course have done you no wrong in particular. The truth is that some religious monarchs, who do not even know where they are going, wish to use you to promote the politico-religious aggrandizements; and deceive you to believe that you will go to heaven after committing both self, and mass murder!

If indeed you aspire to go to heaven, then turn from your wicked ways, and come to Jesus Christ (The Koran even recognizes Him as *Issa Almashihu*), for He alone knows the way to heaven. God bless you for hearing and believing this message.

Indeed, what Saint Paul calls "...zeal without accurate knowledge" in Romans 10, is at work at different levels and degrees, even in other contemporary religions of our time. According to Saint John's Gospel, Chapter 10, the devil's mission is quite clear; which is simply

"....to kill, to steal, and to destroy..." therefore, it is quite easy to identify a man by the type of work he is

committed to doing. Anybody therefore, who is helping the devil in his mission, is of cause a servant of the devil.

Jesus however said *"I am come that they might have life, and have it more abundantly." [John 10:10]*

So those who are pursuing the cause of life, liberty and freedom of mankind, may indeed, be classified as members of God's own army; because God is all about our relationship to Him, and to our fellow human beings; thus living, loving and worshipping God our maker.

Ironically Times interview with some moderate religious Islamic groups discloses that suicide bombing, and the killing of innocent individuals is not consistent with the doctrine of Islamic religion; so we wonder who is deceiving who!

Another thing that struck me about this type of religious zeal, is that most of those involved are predominantly youths of 18 - 20 years, who are apparently assembled quite early in life, and put in Islamic schools, fed and indoctrinated to develop hatred against a particular religious/geopolitical entity. This hatred therefore, grows with them, and culminates in the desire to kill and destroy by way of suicide bombing. They are eventually led to making certain declarations about their goal, which is later played back to intending suicide bombers after they are gone, as a way of inspiring new followers. It is a horrific scenario!

And of course, these guys are never given any option, once they are at the final stages of their training. One Palestinian teenager was however fortunate a couple of months ago, when he was strapped with the death jacket for a kill. However, once he crossed the enemy line, he surrendered and declared that he was not ready to die yet; and so was rescued by the Israelis and disentangled of the death trap.

But even though their modus operandi is already known, yet such operations seem to be on the increase --- deception!
. Of course, you know that the devil is past repentance; so also are his captives! But they are equally doomed to fail.

A little time has been taken to re-examine the degree of deceit inherent in the questionable and uninformed religious zeal of people on the other side of the divide. The idea is to create room for self-evaluation for those on Jesus side --- Covenant men of course! And of course to give others an opportunity to embrace the truth of the Gospel, and be saved, and freed from bondage!

*Above: Some Bible Scholars in action
with the Word of God.*

If certain misguided and brainwashed lot would operate with such a degree of uninformed zeal, what would Covenant people do in a time like these, with all the resources of heaven placed at our disposal? I believe we can be more dangerous! Suicide bombers repose their confidence only on man-made explosives in order to wreck a havoc in society but people of God are imbued with supernatural capabilities that can destroy the works of the devil and his cohorts; but what are we doing with them? Are we really engaging the resources of heaven to stop the enemy's advance? You ask me how can this be possible, and I would tell you to build an altar! If you don't know how to do this, then join a prayer team. The Scripture says:

"...the weapons of our warfare are not carnal, but mighty through God, to the pulling down of strong holds." [11Cor. 10].

The church, being the Custodian of the Covenant, has got the mandate to go and change the world! And when we mention church, you should start your demographic count from two, to three and so on! Yes, two or three is God's quorum to constitute a church. So if you have been looking forward to another Sunday or Midweek worship in order to see a church, you need to change your perspective right now; because you might even have a church in your household already, if there is a minimum of two or three there, who love the Lord!

If two or three can attract His Presence, you can then imagine how God's Presence can be magnified in a larger church congregation who really know Him. It can only be likened to a "cloud of glory!" I mean, that's exactly what it would appear like! Once you get this concept of God's Presence right, then you would not need anybody to tell you to prepare to meet God's overwhelming Presence (with any problem that confronts you), anytime you go to worship on any appointed day of general assembly!

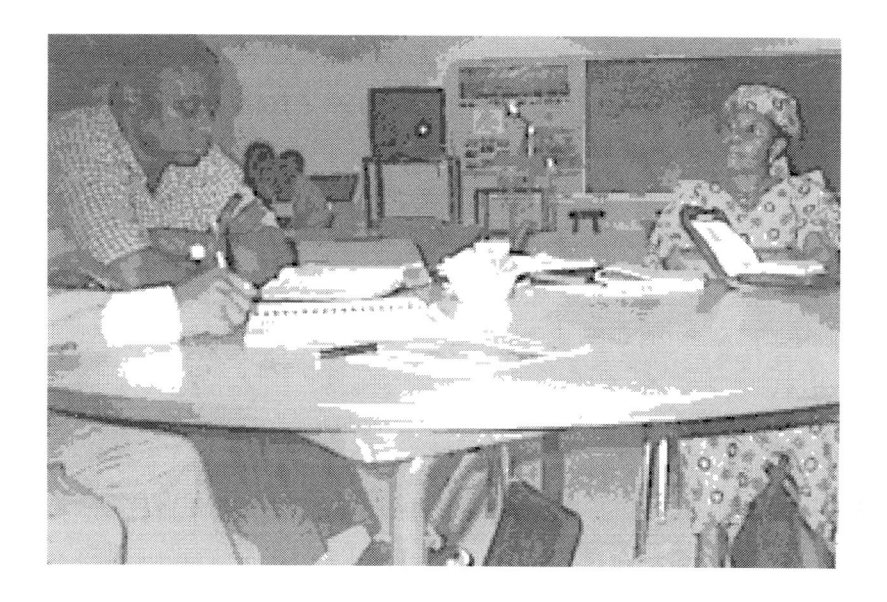

Above: A Bible Study Session at Church.

When you are so prepared, as against the background of your awareness of His Overwhelming Presence, then be sure and ready to receive any miracle! You see, it is because some go to God without any perception of Him, and perhaps little or no expectation from Him, that oftentimes, certain prayers are said over and over again with little or no results recorded.

When a church meets therefore, it does so to do a serious business! The church of God, being the magnet for His Presence, meets to do warfare through prayer and worship. In fact, this is a singular wonderful privilege that believers have! So, you could see why most believers run to be in church at the set time! However, if you wish to get the best out your church sessions you should make sure you draw up clear objectives to achieve, realizing as stated earlier, that you are going to be in God's Mighty Presence!

Then all prayers should be specifically towards pulling down one strong hold of the enemy or the other; similarly, let your praises be aimed at collapsing the 'walls of Jericho' somewhere --- could be in your family circles, in the community, at the national arena or even at international circles; like the global war on terror, etc. To have clear objectives in your prayers and praise worships, speeds up the realization of answers to your prayers.

So where are you, Covenant men of contemporary times? Hear ye now the clarion call to battle. Arise! Arise!! Arise!!! Arise men of God, to your responsibilities. For your roles in times like these are quite peculiar --- Roles the angels would not perform; because they are not the inheritors of the Covenant. You are the ones whom the Scriptures says are made in the image of God! Arise and assume your Godly heritage, and fight. Arise and uphold godliness in the land! In your homes, set the standard; in your businesses, set the standard; in government set the standard! For you have been made pacesetters. Remember it is for this purpose you have been called!

In your closets therefore, go on your knees and call on the Lord! Renew your covenants, and receive fresh anointing and power! Up on your feet, set out to battle! Do warfare in the land
--- Spiritual warfare that is! For the enemy and his captives have infiltrated the land to capture it for themselves. Remember the Lord's command to you is to "Occupy till I Come!" Where are you occupying for Him? Don't give up the fight! Against all manners of ungodliness in the land, don't give up! Sodomy tries to rear its ugly head in the land, don't give up! Against all manner of abuses of my kind in the land, don't give up!

For Godliness remains the required quality to exalt any nation! But it appears some are giving up the fight to uphold my standard! But arise, and don't you give up! For God looks to you to determine the fate of the land! Amen!

If you see the last few lines as a prophetic utterance, then you really got the message! And it is indeed for you to hear, and to run with!

Now, before this chapter is concluded, there are few Scriptures that you should take particular note of whenever you hear about a Covenant man. In Daniel Chapter 11 and verse 32, Scriptures says:

"And such as do wickedly against, the Covenant, shall he corrupt by flatteries; but the people that do know their God, shall be strong and do exploits."

I have often observed the emphasis on two extremes namely, Good or bad, hot or cold, genuine and counterfeit, heaven or hell, etc. With God, you either belong to one end of the extremity, either extremely good or extremely bad, hot or cold! If anybody tells you that a middle point exists, like some religious sects who believe in a place called Purgatory where they say the unsaved go to be made right for heaven, don't you believe it because with God no middle point commitment exists. So if you wish to seek, and live for God, do so with your whole heart; or if you wish to live for yourself or for the world then do so to all extremes. But do not try to put one leg on one extreme, and another on another, and expect to be grouped with people of God when the die is cast! It is one of those deceits of the enemy of your soul, to keep you from living your best for God when you may!

So in the light of the above Scripture, you equally have two categories of people, operating at two different extremes, namely those that do wickedly against the Covenant, and those who show that they know their God and therefore, the Lord enables them to be strong, and to do exploits for Him. These two categories of people are further described in chapter 12 as follows:

"And many of them that sleep in the dust of the earth, shall awake, some to everlasting life, and some to shame and everlasting contempt. (v.2)

Here too, you could see that there is no middle place for middle men, as it were. If you are one of those who believe in a middle place called purgatory, where middle people go to after they are dead before transiting to heaven, then you might be believing an error, because the Bible is the final authority as far as man's eternal destiny is concerned.

Verse 3 goes further to define the blissful experience of those who heeded the clarion call to be wise; and it says:

"And they that be wise, shall shine as the brightness of the firmament, and they that turn many to righteousness

as stars forever and ever. This particular verse also refers to soul winners [See Proverbs 11:30].

As a matter of fact, many Scriptures talk of the characteristics of the Covenant man; but we shall limit ourselves here to a few for purpose of emphasis. However, the next Scripture we shall take a look at is 2Chronicles chapter 7. After Solomon had made a lavish sacrifice and prayer to the Lord, following the completion and dedication of the temple he built unto the Lord, God was provoked to an outburst of pronouncements in favor of his people; and in verses 13,14 God declares as follows:

"If I shut up heaven that there be no rain, or if I command the locusts to devour the land, or if I send pestilence among my people; If my people which are called by my name, shall humble themselves, and pray and seek my face, and turn from their wicked ways; then will I hear from heaven, and will forgive their sin and will heal their land."

Above: Bible Scholars Sharing God's Word!

This Scripture has a number of things to teach us concerning the Covenant man. To begin with, Solomon here, demonstrated his unreserved potential as a covenant man by literally serving as a magnet to bringing down to earth, God's glory and making a positive impact on the lifestyle of the people placed under his care!

Secondly, through his lavish sacrificial offering, God further defined the premium he attaches to his people (those who are called by his name) above all others who are not. God therefore sort of made it abundantly clear to all who might be listening, that as far as He is concerned, the prosperity, peace and progress of the land, depended on the relationship of His people to Him. In other words, if His people wanted the land to prosper and to progress, the only solution to that was the quest for Godliness -
-- seeking Him and submitting to Him period! And of course, it requires God's people to pursue godliness; ungodly people cannot and will not! They may only succeed with the pursuit of religious practices, but not Godliness!

Let me also quickly point out here, that another entity that God recognizes in terms of a nation, is the leadership. He also sees any nation from the point of view of the leader. Where any nation is blessed with a God-fearing man, then that nation is in good hands with the Lord;

because geo-politically, God would deal favorably with such a nation, on account of the leadership. Make no mistake about this!

Needless say that the reverse situation is also true. So, when looking at a comity of nations, God simply sees the figure head of the man who sits at the helm of affairs of each particular nation, either for purposes of assessment and blessing, or for a curse. For instance, Judah and Israel (after the collapse of the northern kingdom) prospered or were depleted and dispersed abroad, depending on how God-oriented their leaders were. Those who loved Jehovah God, prospered tremendously and had victories over their enemies at war fares; but those who

sought after other gods, suffered devastating defeats. I'll give you two close scriptural examples to check out here (Compare the Godly reign of Jotham in II Chronicles 27 and the ungodly reign of his successor, Ahaz in Chapter 28 of the same book).

But there is a point I wish to also highlight here: And that is the possibility of a nation inheriting a double portions of blessings from God.

If God indeed minds His own people (those called by his name), and also equally regards and blesses a nation with Godly leaders, then it means that a nation can be in for a good time where her people are God's people; and where such people unite with their Godly leaders in prayer and fasting; and also where God's people would support their leaders in corporate prayers. If a nation can indeed have her blessings multiplied by a simple unity of believers and leadership, then we should not hesitate to seize such an opportunity! The idea of separating the church from the state therefore looks to me an ungodly inspiration; more so, when a nation is founded on Godly principles.

In verse 14, those who should seek and provide the solution is clearly defined:

"...my people which are called by my name...."

That means, if you are not a member of God's own family as yet, you need to first of all, enter into a covenant relationship with God; and thereafter, you are qualified to be called by His name. And being called by His name, the process starts from inside and manifests outside with time. That is to say, it starts from the spiritual, before it become a physical reality. Thereafter, you grow by developing and practicing a Godly character as inspired by God's holy spirit. If you have already repented of your sins, and invited Jesus Christ into your life as your Lord and Savior, you should now know that it is no mean thing to God; because He distinguishes you so highly amongst ordinary men. Reason: Because, it cost Him his only begotten Son, Jesus Christ to bring you into this Blood-Covenant relationship. Can you then imagine why the Scriptures says that:

"....he that touches you, is touching the apple of His eye." (See Zech. 2:8). Awesome!

Well, my dear reader, this is God's view, and standpoint concerning you. So if you have been folding your hands, not knowing what to do, then you are simply watching precious moments of active service to your Maker and humanity, slip bye!

By the way, your service to God should not be isolated from service to humanity; as a matter of fact, the two are intertwined; because humanity is the center point of God's program on earth. Therefore, if you operate a separate program for God, and a separate one for humanity, then something may be seriously wrong! Sometimes you find people separating secularity from divinity. If you do that, you are simple creating room for the devil, the flesh and the worldliness to manifest; but that will in no way further your spiritual course in times like these. So, by all means, try and harmonize the two to the glory of God, so that in all your activities, you show that you belong to Him.

So, now is the time to wake up to the Covenant realities with your Maker. But in case you have gotten things so mixed up that you no longer know the difference between being called by His name and not being so called, then you might have been knowingly or unknowingly contributing negatively in bringing about the purpose of God for this generation. If that is the case, the process of rededication is still the same: Humble down your-self, pray and seek the face of the LORD, confessing and forsaking every wicked way you have trodden: If you do that, I believe our Merciful God will restore you again, and you would no more, be the same again! Then, and only then will you be renewed and reinforced for His Service again, as God's battle axe man--- a Covenant man in contemporary times!

Above: A Bible Study Group dissect and digest the Word of God.

THE DANGERS OF PARTIAL COMMITMENT TO THE CALL:

It also goes without saying that once you realize who you really are in God, you should have no option than to be serious and committed to the cause. This is very important because an uncommitted lifestyle can cost you your destiny. A life of partial commitment is as bad as no commitment at all; because your next move is highly unpredictable. Worse than that, a life of partial commitment can cut your life short. The name Covenant Man carries with it, a life-long commitment in the Service of the Omnipresent and Omniscient God. That means this call may be more than mere religious titles attached to your name.

I love to hear some men of God, like Dr. Billy Graham, who believes there is no retirement for a man of God; and he practices what he says --- At his late 80's he is still preaching! I see him as one who has a lot of Covenant mentality.

We already said that the Church of God is the Custodian of God's Covenant; Fine! the Scriptures also says:

"...deep calleth unto deep at the noise of thy water spouts... [Ps. 42].

The Spirit of God will always bear testimony to the truth among believers who possess the Spirit of God; because He does not operate in isolation; but speaks to one and also prompts others equally concerning an issue of concern to God. But for you to hear him, you must be operating at the same spiritual frequency with Covenant people! The Church of God is fraught with men with different and varied spiritual gifts, including that of discernment. Yes believers are equipped with the capability to occupy. That means, if we would actually occupy for Him, then the spirit of deceit cannot have any room to thrive amongst God's people!

Having said that, let's take a look at somebody who was described as 'A man of God' but manifestly, not committed to his call, and how he ended up his ministry rather, abruptly. Terrific! The Scripture is indeed wonderfully comprehensive and comprehensible, with every information for a possible successful godly living on planet earth, scripted down for us, to forewarn and equip us for a successful work of ministry!

In the first book of Kings and chapter 13, a certain unnamed man of God was commissioned to go and prophesy against the profane acts of Jeroboam, King of Israel at the time; but the slip-shod approach of the discharge of that assignment, manifests a lot of partial attitude to a serious issue. In verses 2 &3, this unnamed prophet of God proceeded to prophecy against the idolatrous altar set up by the king of Israel, Jeroboam, who eventually reacted sharply, by putting forth his hand to stop the man of God.

The Scriptures however, record that God instantly confirmed the prophecy with signs and wonders, and caused the king's hand which was stretched out against the man of God, to dry up, so that king Jeroboam could not pull his hand back again to himself. Awesome! Also, the prophecy against the profane altar got fulfilled instantly, because it was instantly destroyed.

This unnamed prophet however seem not to set his priorities right before proceeding on this mission. If he did, he might not have messed himself up the way he did. It should be noted that the time of mercy usually precedes the time for judgment. In this scenario, Jeroboam's cup was full and it was therefore time for him to be judged. Apparently the unnamed prophet did not understand things in this order. So, in this state of the fall of God's judgment, Jeroboam had the gut to plead for the restoration of his dried up hand, as if to say God was kidding!

What he should have done was to confess to God, and acknowledge his sin of idolatry, which of course, is a grievious sin before God. But instead, he was more concerned about the restoration
of his hand. And merely by his casual request, the unnamed prophet proceeded to plead on his behalf, for God to restore the man's hand. God of course heard the prayer of the unnamed prophet and restored king Jeroboam's hand. But as it turned out later, this miracle was not to the glory of God, as recorded in verse 33:

"...Jeroboam...made again, of the lowest of the people, priests of the high places" with the restored

hand! And whosoever he would, he consecrated him as the priests of the profane high places (paraphrased).

If you were in the shoes of this unnamed prophet, obviously this would have been the wrong time to make any plea to God on behalf of the ungodly king; or if it became necessary to do so, God's consent should first be sought!

Well, the above scenario was not all that portrayed this prophet as uncommitted with his commission.

But as if that was not enough, this inexperienced unnamed prophet, blatantly toyed with his revelation from God. In verses 9 and 17, of the text, he freely shared privileged visions with everyone (he was such a flippant!) He freely told both the ungodly king (who may or may not appreciate the spiritual value of visions), and the old prophet the basis for his commission, as if to say he was not persuaded about it. The Bible tells us that **'*a double minded man is unstable in all is ways.*'**

Thus the way and manner this unnamed prophet went about this God given commission, portrayed him in a very bad light. You could classify him as a double-minded man; he could rightly be called an inexperienced prophet and therefore, immature in handling spiritual tools of ministry required for such an out-of-field assignment!

After he told all his heart to the old prophet however, then the old prophet had the gut to challenge him and his vision! Friend, there are certain revelations from God, that you should

keep to yourself, until you watch them come to pass. In other words, some privileged revelations through dreams and/or visions are better shared when they become testimonies. To do otherwise, would amount to doing yourself a dis-service, as was the case with this unnamed prophet. In verse 18, we read as follows:

"He (the old prophet) said unto him, I am a prophet also as thou art; and an angel spake unto me by the Word of the Lord, saying, Bring him back with thee into thine house, that he may eat bread and drink water. BUT HE LIED TO HIM." (Emphasis mine).

So, whereas this unnamed man of God from Judah received a specific instruction form God that forbids him from eating bread nor drinking water, nor turning again by the same way that he came by, (v.9) (paraphrased), he now started listening to another message, other than the one he received from God. Someone who just claimed to be a prophet just deceived him with a simple flip of the tongue. This was quite typical of the encounter between Eve and the serpent.

At least, before you believe a message different from the original one you received from God, you should definitely seek God's confirmation. If God spoke to the old prophet, he would much more readily speak to his commissioned man in the field; especially when issues affecting the original mandate is concerned! After all, what does it matter if he had to go back home without taking any food and/or drink, if only to succeed in his God-assigned commission! Obviously, if God thought he needed food and drinks during this mission, surely He would no doubt, have made provision for that!

Worse still, since he had an express instruction to avoid food and drink in the course of this assignment, why not avoid this food and drinks being so subtly offered by an old prophet? At least the scenario of this offer should have aroused some suspicion in the man's mind. Also, it is felt that if this unnamed prophet was more inclined to his spirit than he was to his flesh, he would have discerned that the old prophet had lied to deceived him. But as it turned out, his taste buds had a better part of him! And so without any cross-examination, he was deceived into believing a lie, and eventually proceeded unto the unholy last dinner!

Actually, the attitude of this unnamed man of God here, could fill up ominous volumes if a thorough analysis were to be done. But I believe from a little said of him, we should be able to draw some salient lessons relevant to our subject topic. The lessons to note here, shall be clearer when we take a look at the straight forward disposition of another man of God to his own Commission. But for now, suffice it to say that a Covenant man should always take any assignment or commission from God very seriously because, indeed, your success or failure, and even your longevity depends on how serious you take the work of the Lord here, even if you consider it to be of little significance.

So whether you are a Bible teacher, an usher, a Greeter, a pastor, a financier, a politician, a salesman, a soldier, a police- man, you name it! Whatever you are in society, you should note that God is merely interested in your faithfulness in that job or occupation. If you want to succeed and enjoy a good long life, then make it a point of duty to partner faithfully with God wherever you find yourself. Remember His command to us is to "Occupy till I come." [Luke 19:3].

Secondly, learn not to share your dreams and visions with just anyone you come across. There are certain revelations that indeed should not be shared until they are fulfilled in your life; then they can come from you as a testimony. Sometimes, if you are tempted to share them with people, you discovered that you seem to have abused a privilege! Evidenced in most cases by a disturbed spirit! Thirdly, we should learn to subject everything we hear to a test!

For instance, if somebody tells you that God told him some- thing about you, requiring you to do something, before you believe any bit of that, take some time to seek confirmation of that from God. If you are truly spiritual, and prayerful, definitely God will equally give you a word to confirm or disapprove of such a message. So the chances of believing an error can be rampant, if you don't bring God into the picture of your life's affairs. Of course, the Bible tells us that God is interested in the affairs of men (See Daniel 4:25). If that is the case, then why should we not give God a chance in our undertakings?

Finally, the Scripture says:

"...the Kingdom of God is not meat and drink, but righteousness and peace and joy, in the Holy Ghost. [Rom. 14:17].

That means, if the option is between obeying the Word of God, and going for a party, you don't need any preaching to know the right option to go for! Obedience to God's Word of course!! It would even be better to go without food and drink for a season, or a period in order to obey and please God, than to go for a party and disobey God. You would possibly have another opportunity to eat and drink another day; whereas a singular willful disobedience to the Will of God can mean the end of your very existence on planet earth prematurely, as was the case with the unnamed prophet of our text. Now back to our discussion:

We could see from verses 18 and 19 of 1 Kings 13 that through the use of persuasion and telling of lies, the old prophet eventually succeeded in diverting the direction of the naïve and uncommitted man of God. Then verses 19 and 20 read as follows:

"So he went back with him (the old prophet's emissary) and did eat bread in his house, and drank water. And it came to pass, as they sat at the table that the Word of the Lord came unto the Prophet that brought him back. And he cried unto the man of God that came from Judah, saying: Thus saith the Lord, For as much as thou hast disobeyed the mouth of the Lord, and hast not kept the Commandment which the Lord thy God commanded thee, but camest back and hast eaten bread and drunk water in the place of the which the Lord did say to thee, Eat no bread, and drink no water; thy carcass shall not come unto the sepulcher of thy fathers."

Now look at that! The old prophet who deceived the man of God from Judah through a lying persuasion, has turned around to be used to prophesy about the disobedient and undiscerning man's doom! You have to get it here buddy! God is no respecter of persons; and the Scripture says those who honor Him will he honor, but those who despise Him, will be lightly esteemed. [1 Sam. 2]

Again God's standard is **'the soul that sinneth, that shall die,'** according to Scriptures. Naturally, one would have expected the deceiving prophet to share in the blame, but no! Any Covenant man who toys with his commission is the one that will suffer loss! This should be a serious word of caution to every contemporary covenant person, who goes in the aura that he's got all the time, and all the options in the world to make. You should guard jealously, what you have so that no man would rob you of your crown! [See Revelation 3].

As we know that the Word of God never falls to the ground unfulfilled, verses 23 and 24 speak of the fulfilment of the Word of God:

"And it came to pass, after he had eaten bread, and after he had drunk, that he saddled for him the ass to wit, for the
prophet whom he had brought back. And when he was gone, a lion met him by the way, and slew him and his

carcass was cast in the way and the ass stood by it; the lion also stood by the carcass."

This marked the end of the mission of the man of God from Judah! How sad!!

As a sharp contrast however, compare Jehu's style of executing his own commission from God in 2Kings 9:24-37; 10:6-11. Note that King Jehu was indeed determined to diligently fulfill the Word of the LORD, sentiments apart. Verses 10, 11 states as follows:

"Know now that there shall fall unto the earth, nothing of the Word of the LORD, which the LORD spake concerning the house of Ahab; for the LORD hath done that which he spake by his servant Elijah. So Jehu slew all that remained of the house of Ahab in Jezrell, and all his great men, and kinsfolks, and his priests, until he left him none remaining."

Let's finally see God's opinion vis-à-vis king Jehu and his God assigned commission:

"And the LORD said unto Jehu, Because thou hast done well in executing that which is right in mine eyes, and hast done unto the house of Ahab according to all that was in mine heart, thy children, of the fourth generation shall sit on the throne of Israel."

We may therefore rightly conclude here by saying that indeed your prosperity, longevity and success here will definitely depend on how much your lifestyle fits into God's own pro- gram in bringing His will to be done here, as it is indeed, done in heaven. You ask me why, and I'll tell you that it is because He is the Almighty God, Creator of heaven and earth all the things in them, He is the author and giver of life, He is the

author and finisher of our faith, the Father of our Lord Jesus Christ, (the Soon Coming King), and finally He is our Heavenly Father! Amen.

Review:

- Is it possible that under the New Covenant of the Blood of the Lamb, some could still be destined to perish? Discuss.

- Is it possible for one's name to be erased from the Book of Life? If so, under what circumstances?

- Some still believe that once you are saved, that is it! Do you believe that? Discuss.

- Then what is the plight of those Israelites who fell on the way to Canaan as a result of rebellion.

- How can a man of God stay saved and safe?

CHAPTER EIGHT

"In Understanding Be Men"

"In the first year of Darius the son of Ahasuerus of the Seed of the Medes which was made king over the realm of the Chaldeans. In the first year of his reign, I Daniel understood by books, the number of the years, where of the Word of the Lord came to Jeremiah the prophet, that he would accomplish seventy years in the desolation of Jerusalem. And I set my face unto the LORD God, to seek by prayer and supplications, with fasting and sack cloth and ashes. And I prayed unto the LORD my God and made my confessions..." [Daniel 9:1-4]

Consider buying a piece of equipment, say a lawn mower, or an automobile. When you do that, you are usually supplied with the manufacturer's manual, along with the machine. The idea is to enable you, familiarize yourself with the operational mechanism of your new equipment, so as to enjoy its maximum value as designed by the manufactures. But some would presumptuously jump onto the machine, and begin to attempt to utilize it, after all, it is their money! You might be successful in doing that; but the sad news is that you'd be missing a lot of fun derivable from the machine, had you patiently read up the Manufacturer's manual, which has a full description of the equipment, as well as its entire functional mechanisms. Secondly, you might end up damaging the equipment, or not getting to appreciate its full potentials. Worse still, you may end up forfeiting your manufacturer's warranty as provided in the Manual!

A Covenant man should therefore be a man of books! However, when we talk of books as it relates to a covenant man, do not try to figure out whether you are being asked to go back to the class room for another book-work! Although learning is a life-long business involving a continual use of books, yet when we talk of books here, first of all, our primary focus is the books of the Bible, which I believe you are quite familiar with. Other books that we shall talk about, or recommend, should ultimately point you to the study of the books of the Bible (also known as the Book of Books)! Now, back to our text.

The covenant people of contemporary times

From the text above, Daniel the prophet had searched and researched the books for some vital information concerning the wherewithal of the Jewish nation! In your opinion, which books did he carry out such an extensive research in? I would like to believe they are the Books of the Ancient writings (Scriptures). And of course, through his research, God granted him the understanding of mysteries concerning His people! In this case, he started to figure out when the 70-year prophecy about the desolation of Jerusalem was made initially, and then began to figure out how much of those years might have elapsed, and what was left for Israel to enter into her era of promise. The awareness and inspiration from his study, prompted the prophet to seek the face of the Lord his God, in prayer and supplication, with fasting and mourning, concerning the plight of Israel, the people of God, who had been driven out of God's very Presence on account of their acts of disobedience, and rebellion against their Maker and Deliverer!

The relevance of Books also played a vital role during the reign of King Josiah of the tribe of Judah. Josiah had inherited a devastated kingdom from a godless predecessor, king Amon. Necessity had compelled him to ascend the throne quite early in life, because it was customary for an heir to inherit the throne of his father. And in the case of his father, his reign had been cut short by God because he chose not to walk in the way of the Lord.

Concerning Josiah, the Scripture records that:

".... he did that which was right in the sight of the LORD, and walked in all the way of David his father; and turned not aside to the right hand or to the left." [II Kings 22:2]KJV.

He also had Godly advisors as members of his Governing Council, who apparently had busied themselves trying to review the ruins occasioned by the previous ungodly regime. Verse 8 tells us as follows:

"... Hilkiah, the High Priest said unto Shaphan the Scribe, I have found the book of the law in the house of the LORD, and he read it....And Shaphan the Scribe showed the King, saying, Hilkiah the Priest hath delivered me a book. And Shaphan read it before the king. Verse 11 says:

"And it came to pass, when the King had heard the words of the Book of the Law, that he rent his clothes....And the king commanded ....saying, Go ye, enquire of the LORD for me, and for the people and for all Judah, concerning the words of this book, that is found; for great is the wrath of the Lord that is kindled against

us, because our fathers have not hearkened unto the words of this book, to do according unto all that which is written concerning us."

And this was the word of the Lord that eventually came forth through Prophetess Huldah "Thus saith the LORD God of Israel, Tell the man that sent you to me, Thus saith the LORD, Behold I will bring evil upon this place, and upon the inhabitants thereof, even all the words of this book which the king of Judah hath read: Because they have forsaken me, and have burned incense unto other gods, that they might provoke me to anger with all the works of their hands; therefore, my wrath shall be kindled against this place, and shall not be quenched (Vv. 15-17) KJV.

In verse 18, the prophecy went further to say: "But to the king of Judah, which sent you to enquire of the LORD, thus shall ye say to him: Thus saith the LORD God of Israel, As touching the words which thou hast heard; Because thine heart was tender, and thou hast humbled thyself before the LORD, when thou heardest what I spake against this place and against the inhabitants thereof....I also have heard thee saith the LORD. Behold therefore, I will gather thee unto thy fathers, and thou shalt be gathered unto thy fathers, and thou shalt be gathered into thy grave in peace; and thy eyes shall not see all the evil which I will bring upon this place..." (vv. 19 & 20)KJV.

Also, in chapter 23, we read that the king eventually summoned the elders of Judah and Jerusalem, as well as all the inhabitants of Jerusalem, the priests, the prophets and all the people, both great and small and read out to them, the words of the book of the covenant, which was found in the house of the LORD.

Thereafter, the king covenanted to walk after the LORD, and to keep his commandments and his testimonies and his statutes with all their heart and all their soul, to perform the words of this covenant that were written in this book. And all the people stood to the Covenant! (paraphrased).

That is it, knowledge of the contents of the book, and the willingness to be guided by its contents can make a whole difference between success and apparent failure.

From the foregoing scenario, it appears quite clear that some of the other kings who ended up as woeful failures in both Judah and Israel, had little or no regard for books, and apparently just dabbled into the business of governance; after all, it is only an inherited status, so why bother to study the books of records! This apparent ignorance of the importance of familiarizing themselves with the past records of their predecessors, in order to know why they either failed woefully, or if they succeeded, what they did to achieve such a success! I believe if they were men of books, they could have learned to set their limits, stay on their guard, and allow God to guide their every steps. For some others, their undoing was because they surrounded themselves with ungodly advisors, and never used their sense of discernment to sift the chaff from the actual grain; but apparently, leaned heavily on the ideas of men rather than inspiration from God!

It is also possible, that others resorted to seeking other gods, after they had exhausted all they thought they knew in terms of human wisdom, as opposed to the wisdom of God; perhaps, thinking that doing so would spare them some headache of governance; but only to realize too late that they had gone beyond the point of easy return; and consequently, the judgment of God befell them! Of course, the saying that "If you fail to plan, you unwittingly plan to fail" is quite relevant here!

The need to study the performance of previous achievers, or non-achievers and to learn from their experiences, and to avoid avoidable mistakes, makes it mandatory that a covenant man should be a man of books!

To do otherwise would amount to taking chances in the world of the unknown; and this will not be a wise thing to do. Reason, being that once you get into the arena of power, you are invariably confronted with a lot of competing forces between the devil himself, the world and the flesh, and of course, the urge to do what is right, all demanding attention! But there and then, if your anchor cannot hold, you might find yourself, even going against certain odds. The greatest anchor that cannot fail, is Jesus Christ; and if your desire is indeed to know Him and to please Him as you journey through planet earth, it is important that you are a man of books! In that case, you should make the Bible your best friend, in terms of a reading material.

The Psalmist describes the Word of God as follows:

"The Law of the LORD is perfect, converting the soul: the Testimony of the LORD is sure, making wise the simple. The Statutes of the LORD are right, rejoicing the heart. The Commandment of the LORD is pure, enlightening the eyes....More to be desired are they than gold, yea, than much fine gold: Sweeter also than honey, and the honey- comb." [Psalms 19: 7-8] KJV.

That is it! If you must be a successful Covenant man in your
time, there can be no substitute to being a man of books.

To help you achieve this, an additional reading material titled "Developing Your Reading Appetite" has been provided at the end of this book. It is only meant to provide you with some tit-bits on how to improve your reading habits. So find time to take extra advantage of it!

Review:

- The sin of idolatry contravenes the first commandment, and was a predominant cause for disfavor with God in Israel and Judah. Do you think such a sin is still present amongst God's people today?

- If your answer is positive, Are there any safeguards to the sin of idolatry in contemporary times; and what are they? Discuss.

- Among the kings of Israel and Judah that were described as wicked and idolatrous, from the fall of the northern kingdom, to the period of captivity in Babylon, do you think any preconceived to stray from Jehovah God. If your answer is No, then why was the sin of idolatry such a snare to
them, despite all their physical interactions with God? Discuss.

CHAPTER NINE

Occupy Until I come….."

"And Jesus came and spake unto them, saying, All Power is given unto me in heaven and in earth. Go ye therefore, and teach all nations, baptizing them in the name of the Father, and of the Son, and of the Holy Ghost: Teaching them to observe all things whatsoever I have commanded you: and Lo, I am with you always, even unto the end of the world. Amen."(Matt. 28: 18-20) KJV.

::: So far, we have attempted to discover or rediscover who the Covenant man really is from Scriptural point of view. Once you are certain who the Covenant man is, then the second application should follow sequentially, as to what role he is expected to play in our contemporary times, to help fulfill the Great Commission. To appreciate the contents of this handbook, it is recommended for not only a first reading; but as the need might arise, it might be necessary to read up some particular sections or chapters over and over again until you are in grasp with its message!

However, if you have followed the trend of our discussion so far, you would appreciate the fact that the

Covenant man of our text, is really not a superman! If anything, he is simply an ordinary forgiven sinner, but who is however made extraordinary by the Power of God (Holy Spirit) as it were. Even if you are new on this platform, you should have perceived by now, that God made man in his own image, to function on his behalf on planet earth, and also to help implement his extended programs for mankind!

However, this plan of God was distorted by the devil, sin, and man's rebellion from the divine blue print of God for mankind.

The covenant people of contemporary times

AOL news

High Court Issues Split Decisions on Commandments

Displays Allowed on Government Land, Not Allowed Inside Courthouses

By HOPE YEN, AP

WASHINGTON (June 27) - The Supreme Court ruled Monday that displaying the Ten Commandments on government property is constitutionally permissible in some cases but not in others. A pair of 5-4 decisions left future disputes on the contentious church-state issue to be settled case-by-case.

"The court has found no single mechanical formula that can accurately draw the constitutional line in every case," wrote Justice Stephen G. Breyer.

NEWS HEADLINES:
- Angry Israelis Protest Ahead of Gaza Withdrawal
- Aruba Police Free DJ Held in Missing Teen Case
- Second Teen Attacked by Shark Off Florida Panhandle
- 'It Is a Red-Hot Market' as Crude Oil Tops $60 a Barrel
- In the Year Since Iraq's Sovereignty, 888 GIs Killed

The Supreme Court, pictured above with an activist's makeshift Ten Commandments, issued contrasting opinions.

Watch Multiband Video:
- Major Rulings End Session

Watch Broadband Video:
- Ten Commandments Ruling

Jump Below:
- More Court Rulings
- Background on Court, Justices

Talk About It: Post | Chat

Do you agree with the Kentucky ruling against a courthouse display of the Ten Commandments?
- Yes
- No

Do you agree with the Texas ruling allowing the Ten Commandments monument?
- Yes
- No

[Vote]

206

Suffice it to say that due to His unfailing love for man, God had to start a fresh program of restoration for mankind, and sought for a lead --- someone whose heart is upright. Where God could not find one, he would appointed one; and if he is willing, he would equip him to go! For instance, the Scriptures records that:

"Noah was a just man and perfect in is generations, ...and walked with God" [Gen. 6:9]. In the case of Abraham, the Scriptures also says: "Now the LORD ... said unto Abram, Get thee out of thy country, and from thy kindred, and from thy father's house, unto a land that I will show thee; And I will make of thee a great nation, and I will bless thee, and make thy name great; and thou shalt be a blessing...and in thee shall all the families of the earth be blessed." [Gen. 12:1,2 & 3].

In the case of Moses, the Scripture records as follows: "Come now therefore, and I will send thee unto Pharoah that thou mayest bring forth my people, the children of Israel out of Egypt. And Moses said unto God, Who am I that I should go unto Pharoah, and that I should bring forth the children of Israel out of Egypt?" [Exodus 3:10, 11]

And so on! However, we know that through Moses, God not only brought out the children of Israel from

Egypt, with many signs and wonders following, He also gave us the Ten Commandments in a coded form (in tablets of stone).

Now as compared to Noah's, there is something ominous about the Abrahamic Covenant, which we should take a second look at here, because of its far-reaching implications and relevance to this chapter. It is found in verse three of Genesis chapter 12 and it says:

"And I will bless them that bless thee, and curse him that curseth thee: AND IN THEE SHALL ALL FAMILIES OF
THE EARTH BE BLESSED." (emphasis mine). This aspect of the Covenant was further reinforced in chapter

The covenant people of contemporary times

7,   as   *follows*

"As for me, behold my Covenant is with thee, and thou shalt be a father of many nations. Neither shall thy name any more be called Abram, but thy name shall be Abraham; for a father of many nations have I made thee. And I will make thee exceeding fruitful, and I will make nations of thee, and kings shall come out of thee. And I will establish my Covenant between me and thee and thy seed after thee in their generations for an everlasting Covenant, to be a God unto thee, and to thy seed after thee" (KJV).

From these texts, we could see that God kind of summatively poured out his heart unto Abraham, concerning the destiny of the human race, whom He loves so much. Needless state that the Abrahamic Covenant as we read it here, encompasses the coming of the Messiah, the Lord Jesus Christ. Often you hear that 'Our God is a Covenant-Keeping God.' and that's what He is! Once he gives his word, he kind of stands bye to enforce it. So friend, pray to work within the plan and Covenant of God, for life is only meaningful when you so do! There is just one sad note about king Solomon, as he approached the end of his reign.

The Bible records that:

"....King Solomon loved many strange women, together with the daughter of Pharoah, women of

Moabites, Ammonites, Edomites, Ziddonians, and Hittites; of the Nations concerning which the LORD had said unto the children of Israel, Ye shall not go into them, neither shall they come in unto you: For surely they will turn away your heart after their gods: Solomon clave unto these in love...For it came to pass, when Solomon was old, that his wives turned away his heart after other gods: and his heart was not perfect with the LORD his God, as was the heart of David his father...And the LORD was angry with Solomon, because his heart was turned away from the LORD God of Israel, which had appeared unto him twice....Wherefore, the LORD said unto Solomon, For as much as this is done of

thee, and thou hast not kept my Covenant and my Statutes, which I have commanded thee, I will surely rend the kingdom from thee, and will give it to thy servant." (I Kings 11)KJV.

How art the mighty fallen, one might say! Yes, this is what ungodly women can do!! But man, when God warns us to stay away from a thing, it is for our own good. To disobey the commandment of the Lord, amounts to not only toying with holy things, it also amounts to toying with our well-being here on earth, and of course, our eternal destiny as well! However, on account of the Covenant that God had made with Abraham of old, whose fulfillment was still outstanding; and also for the sake of David, a man after God's heart, God created a rider to a worse- case scenario here!

He said further: *"Howbeit, I will not rend away all the Kingdom but will give one tribe to thy son, for David, my servant's sake, and for Jerusalem's sake, which I have chosen to put my name there."*

A number of issues are worthy of note here. Firstly, God simply is doing this to ensure that His everlasting Covenant of Old, succeeds contemporary generations of the time, despite their waywardness. The memory of the righteous is never for- gotten, as could be seen in the repeated mention of David's name; because he was faithful in keeping God's commandments and statutes. What would you love to be remembered for, as a Covenant man of God? Basically God expects you to be faithful in whatever assignment he has committed into your hands (big or small) and then to be attentive to the voice and/or leading of His Spirit, which lives in you; and also to love and obey His Word.

Another important issue mentioned here is the place of Jerusalem, the choice city, in God's scheme of things and indeed the entire land of Palestine in Middle East. A lot of politicking has been going on in that region in contemporary times. Suffice to say that it is always advisable to take cognizance of God's original plan concerning Israel and the promised land, also mentioned in the Covenant with Abraham. Let's take a brief look at it one more time. It says:

"And I will establish my Covenant between me and thee, and thy seed after thee in their generations for an everlasting Covenant, to be a God unto thee, and to thy seed after thee, the land wherein thou art a stranger, all the land of Cannan for an everlasting possession; and I will be their God." [Gen. 17]. KJV.

Suffice to say that the entire land of Canaan is part of God's Covenant provisions for his people; and it is unsafe to compromise any aspect of this Covenant because God says:

" ...and I will bless them that bless thee, and curse him that curseth thee; and in thee shall all the families of the earth be blessed." [Gen. 12:3] KJV

It means any nation that identifies with the purpose and plan of God for Israel, will get the blessings of God. Some scholars have described the Middle East as the center of the earth. And indeed, that geographical location is God's choice landscape for end time events. For instance, during Christ's earthly three-year ministry, he was wont to pray at the Mount Olives [See Matt. 24:3];

Also, in Zachariah 14:2, commenting about the events of the last days, the day of the LORD, the Scripture says:

"For I will gather all nations against Jerusalem to battle; and the city shall be taken, and the houses rifled...Then shall the LORD go forth and fight against those nations as when he fought in the day of battle. And his feet shall stand on that day, upon the Mount Olives, which is before Jerusalem on the east, and the Mount of Olives shall cleave in the midst thereof toward the east and toward the west, and there shall be a great valley; and half of the mountains shall remove toward the north, and half of it toward the south."

Certainly some of the incidents being described here are still futuristic. That means we should always thread softly on the issues concerning the Covenant package! But more importantly, all Covenant men should be careful, and prayerful when issues concerning God's Covenant promises are at stake because, He says

"....for they that honor me, I will honor, and they that despise me shall be lightly esteemed." [I Sam 2:30].

Now back to our topic: It means if you are a Covenant man of God, then you have the commission to occupy for Him while he's gone temporarily.

You may ask "How can I do that in a complex society like ours? Or yet still, you may say: How can I share my faith in a heterogeneous society like ours? Or How can I do that in a democratic, legalistic society like this? Etc., etc. Friend, I'll tell you, there can be no end to questions and excuses. However, if these are some of your feelings concerning sharing your faith, I should add that it is quite natural to feel that way! But let's read further to find solutions to such negative feelings. And this will take us to discussing the concepts of MIE (maximum impact environment) and PS (power source). In order to easily locate yourself within the MIE context, we shall discuss the PS concept first, so that we have PS+MIE concept to evangelization. Once this concept is properly understood and applied, you would discover that occupying for Him can be an exciting lifestyle of adventure.

Many there are today, who have believed for many years, but yet do not know how to go about sharing their faith with someone; yet if you go close to such people, you find them sounding quite religious and sometime with a lot of head knowledge of Scriptures, but apparently they do not know how to apply and actualize the power in the Word they seem to know! Very often you find such people toying with certain holy things in an attempt to work out solutions to their problems by them- selves (playing God, or helping God as the case may be!) Such people are usually rationalistic when issues of details are at stake, but are invariably guided by human traditions than the Word of God which they claim to believe in. Natural men you may conclude! Possessing the form of religion, but denying the power thereof!!

If this describes your lifestyle, then the good news is that yet another opportunity for your deliverance has come your way. Hold on to this book and read it through! Now let's face it, what shall we attribute this problem to?

Basically, your power source (P/S) as a child of God, is the Holy Spirit; and it is impossible to try to do the work of God successfully with the arm of flesh! You'd just be frustrated out!! And that takes us to the Scriptural injunction in Acts of Apostles Chapter one.

The Apostles had been bewildered after all the mighty miracles they have been opportuned to witness, followed by the unbelievable killing of their Master in a most gruesome fashion. And as He had foretold them, He eventually died, and was buried, and then was resurrected on the third day; and thereafter, HE appeared and reappeared in a glorified body!

And now here they are, escorting their Master to His port of departure from the physical! So they were filled with awe and bewilderment, and indeed, wanted to know more of what to look forward to in the near future!

In such state of the mind, and at such a defining moment, they came up with a crucial question concerning where to go from here; and to ascertain whether or not Jesus would restore the kingdom back to Israel subsequently. But to their Master, (Jesus) that was a far-reaching question indeed to be expected of them, as it was not consistent with His Commission to them, to go and evangelize the world. So, in His response, Jesus felt that this question was wrongly timed; and therefore, proceeded to tell them what was more important and relevant to them at that time, which as you could perceive, was to receive the Power for Sustenance; Power to carrying on with the Great Commission after He was gone!

Let's read from Scriptures here:

And Jesus said: *"But ye shall receive power, after that the Holy Ghost is come upon you; and ye shall be witnesses unto Me both in Jerusalem, and in all Judea, and Samaria, and unto the uttermost part of the earth."* [Verse 8]KJV.

That was a timeless word! So, do you want to serve God effectively and successfully as a Covenant man? Seek to receive and be filled by the Power of God, even the Holy Spirit! Once you are filled with that Power, things will no more be the same with your life of service again ok?. Yes, because once you are filled with the Power of God, then serving God becomes a lifestyle; and when such becomes your lifestyle, you'll find yourself going about it effortlessly in your daily activities. You now become a possessor, and not just a professor of a religious faith! Hallelujah!!

When it becomes your lifestyle, then you are who you are, anytime and anywhere! However, you should also remember that you have not left the earth zone yet; so there might still be time when you would feel discouraged for one reason or another; and then you will find that you'll need to talk to your Heavenly Father for fresh anointing; so you'll find that prayer is another source to power! It is often said that "A prayer less Christian is a powerless one! On the other hand, if you can pray, power is always available to you; for God's ear is inclined to the prayer of His people. Recall when the man of God, Elijah prayed, and how fire came down from heaven, and consumed the sacrifice (in what would appear a naturally impossible circumstance) after the brazen failure of the false prophets of Baal. [See I Kings 18]. Power in Prayer!!!

Then let's take a look at the M.I.E concept: Your maximum impact environment refers to any area or environment where you can exert your maximum influence by reason of your unique position or authority or relationship to that environment. For instance, a man's family should be his primary MIE. Also a Company director hierarchically, is at the helm of affairs in that company; and so can exert his maximum influence down the line. A paid employee can also have his or her place of work as their maximum impact environment. So your MIE can have a direct or indirect implication. To have an effective impact in any given environment, requires the existence of an atmosphere of mutual interpersonal relationship. That way, every member of the given environment can exert a positive impact on the make- up of that environment. That means such an impact may be top to bottom or bottom up once the atmosphere is conducive. The Bible says:

"Ye are the salt of the earth..." [Matthew 5:13].

I believe if every believer serves as the "salt" that you are supposed to be, then you can easily impact your immediate environment successfully irrespective of your status or situation.

Such an impact can also be possible through applied-Godly character; or what is generally called exemplary behavior! (fruit of the spirit).

Often we hear the saying that "Action speaks louder than words." Absolutely true! Where there is a positive conduct, it usually takes less words to impact the given environment for
Christ. So, as you try to impact your environment for Christ, it is advocated that you release your Godly character (the fruit of the spirit) to play a dominant role. The point being emphasized here is that your message to your environment should already be apparent in your conduct and lifestyle.

When we talk of a believer's lifestyle, we are simply referring to the culture of heaven as revealed in the Bible. As a matter of fact, once you acquire this rare characteristic, you will discover that you can equally be successful even in the areas that ordinarily, may be seen as your area of minimum impact environment; and in fact, your minimum or maximum impact environment (as the case may be) will then be a matter of choice, because by reason of your Godly character, invariably, everyone loves to have you around and thus, most barriers are gone! More importantly, you have the favor of God resting upon you! (Anointing!)

Experience, coupled with research have proved that often- times, many wish that their place of employment, or even their immediate family could indeed be their MIE; but unfortunately this has not been so, for want of a Godly character! For instance, what do you expect from a parent who lives a double standard lifestyle --- invariably saying one thing and meaning or doing another. Obviously sooner or later he or she would lose control in that environment! Similarly, a boss who indulges in sexual compromise with his or her employees, or builds his or her business policy on lies and deceit; of course such a person cannot make any positive impact in that environment! Such people would of necessity, need to work hard at recouping their moral bankruptcy through a genuine act of repentance before they can go further.

If the foregoing scenario in any way describes your situation, I would urge you not to despair. In the Bible, Mr. Judas Iscariot was notorious for being impatient in his despair; and of course, he ended up taking the laws in his own hands and died and went to hell. Sad! Obviously, if he had exercised a little patience like Peter did, he might have benefited from a second chance experience through repentance! But unfortunately, he did not! You are therefore, greatly privileged to be reading about his post mortem experience while alive, so you don't go the same route like he did!

On a more serious note, our Heavenly Father is a merciful God, and expects everyone who is not living right, to have a second chance. I'd urge you to go ahead right now, and confess all your sins to Him, and ask for His forgiveness. If you obey, you'd experience the miracle of forgiveness; and you would have your peace of mind back. You see, some people lose out because they feel, Oh I have gone too far against God, Will he also forgive me? The answer is absolutely Yes! He will!!

WHAT IS THE PREDOMINANT OCCUPATION OF THE COVENANT PEOPLE?

May be I should allow you to take a guess here! What actually is the Covenant man's occupation that can enable him to occupy for the LORD? You might say, he had better be a full- time Pastor, or a Bishop, or possibly a Pope? Or maybe, you might think he had better been a Registered Nurse (RN or B.Sc.), a Lawyer, a Teacher, a Soldier, Farmer, or perhaps an author like me, or a full time Pastor, or what have you!

Well if these fit your guess, then I should say your guess is right in one sense, and also wrong in a holistic sense!

Now, let's get things straight: Every man, made of flesh, blood and of course, spirit, are all creatures of God, irrespective of their social status or occupation. That is to say, you are one person, and what you do for a living (occupation) is another thing. That means, your occupation does not make you any more or less than what God says you are! And God says He has made you in his own image That is basic! Also the Scriptures says, and I quote: *"The earth is the Lord's and the fullness there- of; the world and they that dwell therein. [Psalm 24]*.

From the above Scripture, we can easily deduce that both you and your occupation all belong to God. Oftentimes, you find some folks who fancy in bragging about what they are, or what they have achieved, or didn't have.

Thus, some are so proud that they are 7-footer giants, while others feel shy that their stature is small!

Yet some others brag that they possess extra-ordinary intelligence than others; while other are proud about the special privileges they have in life (acquired or inherited).

Well, it is good to be happy and grateful to God for what you have or do not have without prejudice to anyone; but definitely it is wrong for anyone to begin to brag about these things; because, whether you are big or small, rich or poor, etc., etc. it is important to realize that every human disposition come from our Heavenly Father, who made everything as they are for His own pleasure. I would rather have you see things that way, as if seeing things with "an eye of God", who loves to have variety of things, and diversity of nationalities, thereby having all the characteristics of his creatures and creations represented everywhere, and complementing each other in the knowledge and fear of God! If you actually believe in life hereafter, in the Kingdom of Heaven, then you can't afford to see things differently!

I think this idea is also true of the occupations! It also means depending on the artificial value you add to yourself through the process of schooling or training (because obviously, no one is born with any skill;) and then you occupy as an accountant, or a banker, carpenter, doctor, engineer, or farmer, you name it; so long as it is a legitimate and legally definable occupation. Then ideally, you should see yourself as occupying such an occupation for God, whom it has pleased to fix you there.

Some often try to excuse themselves from serving God by defining their jobs as either secular job (where God' Name is prohibited!), or a religious job (where God's Name is authorized!) So invariably you find people trying to put up with different characters for each job description or "job definition!" These are some of the deceptions of the enemy, whose intention is to deny you the opportunity to serve and be a representative of the Living God even in your occupation!

Now, let me announce to you that the time is now ripe for you to use every time at your disposal, to serve God, because all the time and opportunities belong to Him. Therefore, all those 'statutory and psychological' mentality should now begin to give way to your knowledge of God's Word, which is the truth! Of course, as a Covenant man that you are supposed to be, you should have built up enough resource base (Godly character) over the hours, days or years that you have known Him. If my assumption is right, would you tell me, how possible it might be, to temporarily put off your character, which actually is your personality, simply because you are in one secular environment or the other, only to try to put it on again, when you are at home or at church? I think this to me, is impracticable. If anyone tries to do that, then that would amount to a life of hypocrisy; or per- haps such a person has not yet repented of his old way of life.

On a serious note, any job that presents you with such a condition, would not be a good one for you as a Covenant Man. In my opinion, a job that would force you into a life of hypocrisy is not worth taking. The point being made here is that the time you are at work, is equally the time you should demonstrate your Godly character (fruit of the Holy Spirit) by putting it to work, thereby making a positive impact on someone's life; brightening your own little corner with the presence of God in you. With this awareness, you should go ahead, and make your workplace your immediate mission field. Yes, indeed, your maximum impact environment!

What the Scripture says in Romans 8 is equally challenging here. It says: **For the earnest expectation of the creature waited for the manifestation of the sons of God." (v.19).**

Do you know that today, as always, the whole world is earnestly watching out for those peculiar men and/or women, who are different from the rest of the people; those who of course, have been born of the Spirit of God, and are only concerned about doing good because of the nature of God in them. Any time you put the character of God in you to work, by doing kind deeds to someone, you are simply bringing this Scripture into a positive fulfillment. For instance, think of the beautiful aura that surrounds you when you care to drop a few coins in the waiting hands of a beggar in the street, or whenever you do any act of kindness to someone in need! But how often, we let such precious opportunities to slip bye!

One day as I drove through a bye way in the city one beggar man showed up as the traffic light turned red for vehicles to stop. He quickly stretched out his empty can, expecting to have coins dropped into the empty can. However, something prompted me to dish something more than a coin to this unsuspecting man; and as I reached out in my pocket, fortunately there was a careless dollar bill there; and before the lights turned green for vehicles to move again, I quickly squeezed it into the man's hands; and as I drove off, I noticed as great sense of joyful surprise. The man was filled with awe! Apparently, he never expected to get what he received. And of course, I too was filled with a sense of fulfilment. And I have learned, rather than dump all the large offerings into the offering plate, sometimes when led, to look out for such rare opportunities to minister this way, to unsuspecting, but needy beggars. We should always look out for ways we can do something to make a difference in somebody's life especially in a surprising and impactful manner. By so doing, we would be occupying for the LORD while we still await His Return. Who knows? Perhaps such a gesture might turn out to be the last opportunity to impact a life! May be also, it is for such rare ministries that some of us have been called of God (Saved to Make a Difference in our Father's World --- SMDFW). If you believe this, say a loud Hallelujah!

If indeed you have been called of Him; and if you believe that the Lord has indeed, made you the light of the world (Matt. 5:14) then let us arise and shine, so that eventually we'll begin to outshine the powers of darkness now at work every nooks and cranny of t, trying to take overtake our territories! But as we know, one thing is certain: Once the light comes in, the darkness has no option than to vanish, BECAUSE DARKNESS CANNOT RESIST THE LIGHT! This is the greatest challenge of our time for all Covenant People!

WHAT OTHER OPTIONAL ROLES ARE THERE FOR COVENANT PEOPLE?

Some would want to play the gentleman believer approach, or the secret believer mentality, so that they would play it safe, hurt no one's feelings, talk to no one, (even when they have a divine command to do so for good); mind your own business, etc. Fine! So are there any optional lifestyle for covenant people in the light of the Lord's Great Commission? Of course, the answer is absolutely "NO." You see, the Word of God is a timeless, yet a time-sensitive thing. This explains why you find such urgent appeals for a Now-posture in Scriptures. In II Corinthians 6, the Scripture makes this urgent appeal to *listeners:*

"For he saith I have heard thee in a time accepted and in the day of salvation have I succored thee: Behold now is the accepted time: behold now is the day of salvation."

The appeal of God always expects a NOW response because if you wait or procrastinate, either the appeal will become more difficult to accept, or it will no longer be there for you in particular. It could also mean that the time comes when the appeal of God is no more valid; and then, it will be too late to do anything about it! But if you want your response to make useful and beneficial appeal unto God, then you've got to adopt a "NOW approach in your response patterns to things of God.

On a more serious note, all Covenant men should see them- selves as a privileged lot, because our God whom we have to do with, is an Awesome God, even though He reserves a special place for man, whom the Scriptures tells us that He made in His own image, and whom He crowned with glory and honor! [See Psalm 8]

At the same time, He loves to honor those who honor him, as we read in II Sam 20.

The people of Judah and Israel who refused to give God their total devotion, had to lose their original place in the scheme of things, and consequently, God withdrew His protection over them; and they had to be taken captive in Babylon; and at the fullness of time, God had to use a godless king to do their job, by decreeing and implementing the rebuilding of the desolate Temple in Jerusalem, (the City of God). And eventually, those who lost their first place ended up playing a second fiddle under the direction of an ungodly king! [See Ezra 1-6]. Too bad!

A similar scenario was also replayed during Christ's earthly ministry on earth. One day people saw Christ coming, and approaching the Mountain of Olives, at the east of Jerusalem; the Scriptures records that "....the whole multitude of the disciples began to rejoice and praise God with a loud voice for all the mighty works that they had seen; saying, Blessed be the King that cometh in the name of the Lord: Peace in heaven, and glory in the highest." However, as it were, the Pharisees among them who did not like what was going on, and perhaps thought the disciples were constituting a nuisance in society, not knowing the mind of Christ, urged Him to rebuke the disciples who were shouting and praising God. But they were wrong!

In His response, Christ surprised them: The Scripture records as follows:

"...and He answered and said unto them (the Pharisees) If these should hold their peace, the stones would immediately cry out." [See Luke 19:37-40]

That is it! From the foregoing passage, you could see that though the program of God goes slowly at His Will, yet it also goes steadily; and no one, can stop or frustrate His plan or purpose; because if it becomes necessary, He can use any available instrument, (even stones, or unbelievers) to fulfill His purpose. But Covenant Men should not allow that to happen!

Another important lesson here, is that if God so willingly appoints you to serve His purpose, (big or small), then you should see it as a great privilege!

That means you should give it your whole attention, because our God is an Awesome God!

This issue of time once stirred my sensibility, and a little research that followed revealed a lot to me, some of which I share with you here. You see, every human activity is hinged up on time, and it requires time to validate any human activity under the sun. Once time roles bye into eternity, either with or without a scheduled activity, everything becomes history. What

a wonderful gift we have from God --- Time! Think of any conceivable event that is schedule to take place at a certain future time. Initially, you would think oh, this event is still far in the future. But sooner than later, the "D" Day arrives, and in a couple of moments, that scheduled event is now past and forgotten, as if it never occurred!

Some Bible scholars have referred to the word, "History" as short for "His Story," just like some described the word, "woman" as short for "womb man" and I absolutely agree with them. These ideas are quite credible to me because they fit into Scriptural context. In the case of the theory about History for "His Story" meaning God's Story, I fully agree, because God causes time to evolve through the evolution of night and day, time and seasons, weeks and months, years and decades, and of course, centuries! And therefore, everything that chronicles around time can be credited to Him! That means the concept of His Story should be well taken!

Now to think of it, if this re-discovery is indeed the reality about God and time, then why do some people place so much emphasis on their business appointments, which is only validated by time which is under God's control, and Who causes the next business opportunity to come bye? For instance, you find some men in church; and instead of forgetting themselves for a while when they are before God, they are busy checking on their time!

There and then, I came to a quick realization of what the Scripture says about time, and I was shocked about the awesomeness of the Word of God! Let's go there right away: It says:

"Now listen, you who say, Today or tomorrow we will go to this or that city, spend a year there, carry on business, and make money. Why? Do you not even know what will happen tomorrow! What is your life?

You are a mist that appears for a little while and then vanishes. Instead, you ought to say, "If it is the Lord's will, we will live and do this or that. As it is, you boast and brag. All such boasting is evil." (James 4:13)NIV.

Another Scripture concerning God and time is equally interesting; and it says: *But he that doeth the will of God abideth forever (1John 2:17)KJV.*

Put together, it means without any exception, everyone should not only seek to serve the LORD, but it is also every- one's responsibility to acknowledge and reverence HIM. That equally means, seeking and serving Him, is never an optional issue! And this equally places a greater responsibility upon all who have been birthed within the Covenant Provisions of God, (Covenant Men that is) to wake up and assume the full responsibility of their birthright, by obeying the Divine Command, to 'OCCUPY UNTIL I COME' and help change the world!

Any privilege received, goes with it, a corresponding responsibility to be performed. Having said that, it is my pleasure to declare to you, to look to no one else for the covenant man; rather, realize now, that YOU ARE THE COVENANT PERSON OF OUR TIME! So Covenant Man, Arise!!!

REVIEW:

- What is the time limit to the injunction to "Occupy till I come.?"
- What is the relevance of our occupations to this divine command? Discuss.
- Is it any easier to occupy in specific occupations than in others?
- Why do you think the Lord actually wants us to occupy until He comes?
- Do you think to occupy is more of a corporate exercise rather than individual? So how best do you think this can be achieved?

CHAPTER TEN

Show Forth The Light?

"The secret things belong unto the LORD our God: but those things which are revealed belong unto us and to our children for ever, that we may do all the word of this law."
[Deut. 29:29]

The previous chapter, titled "Occupy Till I Come" was primarily an injunction of our Lord Jesus Christ to his disciples, of which by implication, you and I are one today, or are supposed to be one. May be you have not considered what a great privilege it is to be asked to occupy the stage as a *defacto* owner, on behalf of the *de'jure* owner of the stage. Ordinarily, when someone tells you that kind of a thing, it implies that obviously, that person knows you, and believes that you can represent him very well ideologically and in practice because you operate on identical frequencies; in other words, you are one with him. I am sometimes given to believe that the reason most believers take certain issues of faith for granted is because they received everything free of charge!

But on a serious note, holders of such a view, should equally realize that it cost God the life blood of His only begotten Son to secure your salvation; so even though it was a free gift to you, it was not actually cost-free! Usually when a man is not sure of his status in a given scenario, you invariably find him switching camps. He does that because he does not know the grave implications of a half-hearted commitment, either to himself, or to his silent admirers. *(The implications of a half-hearted commitment was discussed in chapter four).* It is important to note that issues of faith are not bed of roses; they often entail a serious attention to details that invariably involve a life or death implications; this is especially so, when they play a role in determining one's eternal destiny. If you are a Covenant person, or you wish to be one, then you would need to ask the Lord God to help, order your steps accordingly. When that happens, do not under-rate the importance of your role in God's vineyard. Once you come over to God's side through repentance and/or rededication, then everything you do or say, begins to carry weight!

In academics for instance, it is usually counterproductive to carry out a research in an area that has already been researched upon before.

Therefore, before you step out to do a study or research on any particular phenomenon, your first step normally, is to go and take a look at the state-of-the-art in that particular field of endeavor, so as to ascertain what areas that have not been addressed or covered by a previous research effort. After that, you then pro- pose your project topic for approval by your supervisor. These first steps are usually very important; and I believe you know why: To avoid a waste of time, limited resources, and of course efforts too; and more importantly, because if you dare go ahead without these preliminary steps, you would end up not achieving a credible research project, because the outcome of your research is already in existence.

In our everyday scenario, you'd agree that a man's day is full of issues of the day that compete for his attention; and so a wise person who wants to make the best use of time, would definitely not go out looking for extraneous problems to add, when in actual fact, his hands are full of unresolved ones; except he is done with them! Some have suggested that the term "problem management" would fit properly as a synonym for life! How often you hear the idiomatic expression "let sleeping dogs lie;" with dogs here representing unscheduled problems. Indeed, the whole world, since the fall of man, is full of problems and problem management; and therefore, it is expected of people of the Covenant, to join hands with God to be problem solvers, or a problem manager rather than a problem maker. If you assume this role, you'd notice that you'd be helping to give a sense of direction to human issues on planet earth, where you have been given a divine mandate to "occupy...."

Having said that, I'd like us to take a look at Jesus' approach to a certain complex human problems that came to his attention. Once we grasp this concept, then you would have made a step forward in your knowledge of anthropology!

The scenario is the familiar case of the healing of one formerly blind man, called Bartimaeus.

Let's read:

"And they came to Jericho; and as He went out of Jericho with his disciples and a great number of people, blind Bartimaeus, the son of Timaeus, sat by the high way side, begging. And when he heard that it was Jesus of Nazareth, he began to cry out, and say, Jesus, thou son of David, have mercy on me. And many charged him that he should hold his peace. But he cried the more a great deal, Thou Son of David, have mercy on me. And Jesus stood still, and commanded him to be called. And they called the blind man, saying unto him, Be of good comfort, rise; he calleth thee. And he casting away his

garment, rose, and came to Jesus. And Jesus answered and said unto him, WHAT WILT THOU, THAT I SHOULD DO UNTO THEE? THE BLIND MAN SAID UNTO HIM, LORD, THAT I MIGHT RECEIVE MY SIGHT. AND JESUS SAID UNTO HIM, GO THY WAY; THEY FAITH HATH MADE THEE
WHOLE. And immediately, he received his sight, and followed Jesus in the way." (emphasis mine) [Mark 10:46-52] KJV.

I have taken time to put down the whole scenario about this Man of Faith Bartimaeus; (former Blind Bartimaeus) because this is the crux of the mater! Some believers seem to find pleasure in going about to figure out the unannounced problems in people's lives (marriages and homes inclusive). I discovered of late, that some do this, not for the purpose of adding such problems to their prayer lists, but rather because they find pleasure in discussing them amongst their gossip groups. This is most unfortunate! Such people seem to be contesting God's word that says "Secret things belong to God......" You see, I have come across a number of good-looking people, who have no control of their tongues and often allow their tongues to get them into serious trouble. Some have ruined their homes by uncontrolled talking and gossiping; and needless state that such people can hardly keep their friends because of the poison on their tongues! If you are in this habit, I believe it is either because you do this ignorantly, or you are controlled by some negative powers beyond your control, not knowing the Scriptures, as it were! If you are in this group, then here comes another opportunity for your deliverance! I believe, as you see the inherent evil that lies along that pathway, you should not waste a moment to repent and retrace your footsteps.

Now, back to 'Man of Faith' Bartimaeus. (I believe this should now be his appropriate name, since he has been healed of his blindness!) Friends, I feel the message in this Scriptural passage is overwhelming!

Firstly, although physically handicapped by way of blind- ness, this man was quite wide awake spiritually, and quite well connected to the events of the day around him; and in this agile and attentive posture, he heard that the Guest of Honor in town was Jesus of Nazareth whom he had apparently heard so much about, as a miracle-working God. You could imagine Bartimaeus tightening his belt, and adjusting his faith upwards, to receive! You could also imagine him say to himself, "I won't miss this opportunity to recover my sight this time around!" Also, you could imagine him sharpen his ears, to discern the type of noise that would herald Jesus' arrival in town! You could also imagine him decide how he would shout to the

The covenant people of contemporary times

limits of his lungs, until he attracts attention!! Now, looking at this scenario, you would agree with me that Bartimaeus was quite prepared, and determined; as if to say to himself, "I am not going to miss my miracle today!"

Being blind, obviously he depended more on sound waves; so once he suddenly heard the noise that heralded His coming, he then started his unstoppable faith outburst: "JESUS THOU SON OF DAVID, HAVE MERCY ON ME!" Note here also,
that his description of Jesus was quite informed; so he did not mince words. Rather, he used an accurate description of one of Jesus' Scriptural Names "Son of David."

Secondly, despite men's effort to dissuade him, he persisted in his desperate cry of faith; and eventually, despite the pressing crowd and the attendant noise, his cries caught Jesus' attention and He commanded that the blind man be brought to him. And as a further evidence of his resolute faith, the Scriptures record that "…he cast away his garment, rose and came to Jesus." Fine! But did the matter end there? Of course, not! Now, I want you to pause momentarily and think it over. Just imagine yourself in Bartimaeus' shoes, and under the circumstances he found himself that day. How do you think you would react to the situation? Well, whatever you feel about it, please note that you equally need Bartimaeus' kind of faith, in order to have your breakthrough on your own peculiar issues. God is always dis- posed to release miracles to his children but oftentimes you have to prove by your faith (expressed in words and action) that "I am a candidate for a miracle!"

Of course, testimonies abound of how some Godly women started shopping for their baby stuff, even before their babies were conceived in the womb, as an act of faith! And of course, they all had their expectations met!!

There is a popular saying that "Faith honors God, and God honors faith." You see, when you are a Covenant person, you'd often find fun exercising your faith for certain covenant blessings. When you exercise your faith within the context of God's promises, it is like claiming the blessing by faith, before it actually arrives! The undersigned has experienced this many times, and would love to have it as a life style! You see, provided you are acting within the provisions of God's Word, you are in order! It, in no way depicts being covetous; rather, you are, in cherishing faith, saying, I can't wait to have my covenant blessing! And invariably, it is yours.

To boost your faith in approaching the throne boldly for miracles, try and meditate on such Scriptures as Psalm 84:11: *"For the LORD God is a Sun and a Shield: the*

LORD will give grace and glory; no good thing will he withhold from them that walk uprightly."

Then Romans 8:32: *"He that spared not his own Son, but delivered him up for us all, how shall he not with him freely give us all things?"*

There are so many Scriptures that depict God's positive dis- position to give you all the desires of your heart, consistent with His Word; but your faith approach is a very important factor for this breakthrough! Yes, it plays an important role even in classifying the blessing you eventually receive, either as a "mercy- drop" or "showers of blessing!"

Now let's pause and see how Jesus Christ addressed this blind man's issue here. I think we should have a whole lot to learn from the Son of God and Son of Man, in His approach to problem-solving. I believe you could not imagine any better teacher on issues of human problem than the Maker Himself! Once we can grasp His approach here, we save ourselves from a lot of unnecessary worries about certain aspects of unresolved social problems as it relates to man. If you saw someone who cannot see, I believe human instinct and emotion would make you feel and believe that automatically, this man's greatest need is to have his sight back; and if you were capable of meeting such a need, obviously you would do just that without asking any questions about it. But you might be wrong! This is because, as a human being, the blind man may have other priorities that are more important to him, hidden from the eyes of men!

You see, as a human being, God has given you a will to exercise during your sojourning here on earth, and of course He respects the exercise of your will; and needless state equally, that you are accountable to Him as to how you exercised this will power in the end. So when you hear Scriptures that say "….It is appointed unto man to die, and after that, comes judgment….." That is it! You will one day give an account of how you played around with this will power of yours. Well, enough on *the exercise of your will p6wer* for now!

: When Bartimaeus stood before Him, does it strike your imagination why the All-knowing God did not suddenly arrive at a conclusion that 'since this man is blind, surely, to see, would be his immediate compelling need; and then proceed to make him to see?' "Of course Not" is the answer! Instead, the first million dollar question Jesus asked the man was: "What will thou that I should do unto thee?" Until this "million dollar" question was satisfactorily answered, no further move was to be made about the man's situation. So

Jesus waited to hear the man's order of priorities; because, although Bartimaeus' defining moment had come, it still remained his prerogative to say what he wanted to achieve with such a rare opportunity! Friend, once you grasp this concept of God, then you have graduated; and you have grasped the whole concept of this chapter.

Well, thank God that the blind man equally had his priorities ordered from the word "go;" and that is to receive his sight! So without wasting any time to think about it, he quickly said it out: "That I might receive my sight." And equally without wasting any time, Jesus proceeded to grant him his request by saying "Go thy way, thy faith hath made thee whole."

Can you see that? So next time you come across a man or woman, even if such a person is physically handicapped; following Jesus' example here, don't you ever assume that you know it all, as far as their problems are concerned. First of all, find out what the person's priorities are before you begin offering your assistance or sympathies, in case that is your objective.

This problem is rampant amongst contemporary believers. It is so much that you might classify it as "a sin of the saints." Some just cherish dwelling on people's undisclosed problems, that it has become habitual to them. If you are there, my prayer is that before you drop this book, that God will have mercy on you, and deliver you from this habit in Jesus Name (Say a loud Amen!) But note that to turn from an evil habit is also a function of the exercise of will power. That means, you have to realize that this habit you cherish so much is evil; and therefore to make up your mind to repent and to come out of it. Once you have taken that preliminary step, you can then ask for God's help. Usually there are steps to receiving from God which everyone should be familiar with. Of course, you don't stay with an evil habit and still expect your prayer to be answered. First cleanse the 'house' through repentance and confession to God then you would have opened the doorway to heaven!

Now to cap up Bartimaeus' encounter with Jesus, the Scripture records that "And immediately, he (Bartimaeus) received his sight, and followed Jesus in the way." When calling Bartimaeus next time, therefore, I think his appropriate name should no longer be qualified with the word "Blind" rather the more appropriate word should be "Man of Faith" Bartimaeus!

THE EVILS OF A LIFE OF GOSSIP:

So far, we have seen from the foregoing, that God respects the exercise of our will power, often expressed by way of ideas, opinions and actions. This equally may imply that you should not assume that anybody has a problem or need that he has not declared to you, or made public one way or the other; not to talk of discussing such assumed problems with others. If indeed you feel so concerned about anybody's apparent but undeclared need(s) or problem, then at best, let such a knowledge end up only in your personal prayer list, for intercession purposes only. This is because, to announce another person's undeclared problem, even as a prayer request, except with the person's consent, amounts to a gossip of a sort. So you are warned, STOP IT!

You see, for a believer who wants to make heaven, little things can be very important to him or her. Anyone who thinks he can go about life carelessly here, had better watched it! Else, you may get carried away by avoidable errors of other men and with disastrous consequences. We know that someday, the Rapture is going to take place, when believers who constantly respond to the prompting of the Holy Spirit, to drop little sinful habits, or even bad companions, that are capable of hindering your walk with God, will be taken away! I'm sure you know that there are some who will be left behind to face the rule of the anti-Christ? Make sure you are not in that company of people today.

What do you think will result in such leaving behind of some "believers?" Of course the answer is what we are discussing in this chapter: Little unconfessed, and unforsaken sins! Little acts of un-forgiveness, etc. I do strongly believe that our Loving Heavenly Father has made every provision for everybody to make heaven; and that is why He made all the provisions for us, and on top of that, gave us His Holy Spirit to abide with us after our Lord Jesus Christ went back to heaven.

It also means, so long as you'd co-operate with the leading of the Holy Spirit on all issues of life and righteous living, your place in heaven is as good as secured! (Say a loud Amen!) In summation: If you want to make heaven, here is your of To-Do List: First of all, believe the Gospel: Confess your sins to God, and welcome the Lord Jesus Christ into your heart, as your Lord and Savior. After that you need to know the Word of God. And to achieve that, find a Bible believing and teaching church or fellowship nearest to you, where the Word of God is preached and taught. Make it a habit to move with people of God; in the process, seek to be filled by the Holy Spirit. When that happens, then you are fully equipped! Begin to tell others about your born-again experience, and how they too can be prepared for heaven!

IS THE SIN OF GOSSIP A NOVELTY?

The answer is a capital No! From the Bible account, the first sin of gossip and punishment for same dates back to the time of Moses' Ministry era! During this time, some took this man of God for granted, and began to gossip against him. God showed up on behalf of Moses. And of course, they did not go scot-free! You see, all unhealthy, and therefore ungodly habits are the lifestyle of the world; and that's why the Bible warns us that "He who makes himself or herself a friend of the world by copying their sinful habits, automatically becomes an enemy of God." (1Jn.2:15-17) (para-phrased). Let's also see what the Scripture says about the sinful habit of gossip:

"And Miriam and Aaron spake against Moses because of the Ethiopian woman whom he had married; for he had married an Ethiopian woman. And they said: Hath the LORD indeed spoken only by Moses? Hath he not spoken also by us? And the LORD heard it.....And He said, Hear now my word: If there be a prophet among you, I the LORD will make myself known unto him in a vision,

and will speak unto him in a dream. My servant Moses is not so, who is faithful in my house. With him will I speak mouth to mouth even apparently, and not in dark speeches and the similitude of the LORD shall he behold: Wherefore then were ye not afraid to speak against my servant Moses? And the anger of the LORD was kindled against them; and he departed. And the cloud departed from off the tabernacle; and behold Miriam became leprous, white as snow; and Aaron looked upon Miriam, and behold she was leprous. And Aaron said unto Moses, Alas my Lord, I beseech thee, lay not the sin upon us, wherein we have done foolishly and wherein we have sinned. Let her not be as one dead of whom the flesh is half consumed when he cometh out of his mother's womb...." [Num. 12] KJV.

As we consider this problem now, someone may be saying in his heart, may be Miriam did that because she was not a believer! Well, you don't know Miriam before so I don't expect you to say that! But be that as it may, I traced Miriam's Resume, to discover where the Bible describes her as a Prophetess! [See Exodus Chapter 16]. The point there is that anybody can fall prey to a sinful habit, if you should toy with it. And of course the Bible warns us that **"....Let he who thinks he stands, take heed lest he fall." [1Cor. 10:12]**.

However, I am much more interested here in what a Covenant man or woman may do to stay spiritually on top all the time. And we shall pick just three Biblical clues here: The first panacea to a fall is found in John's Gospel, chapter 8, where Jesus says: "If ye continue in my Word, then are ye my disciples indeed; and ye shall know the truth, and the truth shall make you free." You should continue to be a student of the Word of God; and after your study, make time to meditate on the Word, and let the Spirit of God interpret the Word to you. Because, to know is to do!

Another helpful hint is found in Hebrews 10:24&25 that says: *"Let us consider one another to provoke unto love and to good works: Not forsaking the assembling of ourselves together as the manner of some is; but exhorting one another; and so much the more, as ye see the day approaching."* The importance of constant fellowship with other believers, to give thanks, pray, study the Bible cannot be overemphasized!

Lastly, the third one is found in II Timothy 2:15, which says: *"Study to shew thyself approved unto God, a workman that needeth not to be ashamed, rightly dividing the word of truth."*

After a group study session, you should still make time to spend alone, studying and meditating on the Word of

God, thus fashioning out your own tools for ministry based on knowledge of the Word! It goes without saying that you should also make a good selection of Christian literatures that you should 'consume' within specific periods. By so doing, you read up the state of the art from men of God in different fields of ministry! This also enables you to avoid certain enemy traps already explored into and discovered!

I wish to conclude this chapter by quoting from another Scripture which challenges everyone to a life of maturity with issues of understanding. It says:

"Brethren, be not children in understanding; howbeit, in malice be ye children, but in understanding be men." [1Cor.14] KJV.

When the Scriptures talk of maturity, it is simply talking of knowledge of the Will of God, and the ability to put it to work. Of course, no one can boast of knowledge of Scriptures or the Will of God, when his lifestyle is preaching a contrary message; because that would be a terrible contradiction; and a horrible mixture!

On the contrary, all Covenant People, as sons and daughters of light, should give expression to the light of God in them, and let it outshine the darkness of the world around them. For never on earth, can darkness resist the light when it begins to shine; but on the contrary, at the approach of light, darkness will begin to flee and eventually vanish away! As a Covenant Man, that is your role and your portion in Jesus Name. Amen!

Review:

- What is an average person made up of?

- How does the Bible describe the making of man?

- Car manufacturers produce spare parts for replacement of defective ones.. Do you think as the Maker of man, God can equally replace human parts damaged by accident, disease or human (doctor's) error?

- If your answer is yes, give some instances with some living testimonies.

- If God is the Maker of man, then whose opinions should be taken more seriously concerning his product? Explain.

- How do you think God views the issue of gossip?

- What is the panacea for backsliding?

CHAPTER ELEVEN

**DEVELOPING A READING APPETITE

Introduction:

Developing an Appetite for Reading is the next in the Developing Your Appetite series.

If you take an imaginary survey of any contemporary city's consumption patterns, you tend to discover that only an insignificant proportion of consumers pay regular visits to the book-shops and libraries where you find books on diverse topics in different fields of endeavor. This author placed some rare books in a traditional African Store as a test case, but though the books were carefully displayed, yet they survived the watching eyes of buyers for several months! That was typically indicative of a community with a zero appetite for reading!

A recent visit to some popular bookshops in the city made a deep impression on my mind, as I tried to visualize an array of published reading materials – books and magazines, etc., so beautifully designed and displayed; and I wished I could acquire as much of them as possible for my library, for a gradual consumption. Typically, the array of books I saw, looked to me, like edible gold waiting for patronage! But alas, only very small percentage of the city's consumer population go after them, as compared to patronage to other consumer goods stores, like the one mentioned above.

I then tried to imagine the degree of apparent ignorance in the city, and how such lives could have been positively impacted, if there could be positive changes in reading habits. Suffice to say that the books are available; but patronage is not anything to write home about! The picture of this ugly scenario, makes the above title not only community-friendly, but very important.

However, I made a discovery recently when I paid a visit to some Bible Study groups where a reading culture is being revisited. In one of the Family Classes, every participant is encouraged to purchase a copy of a choice title, which serves as a class discussion material; and you could see the reading culture being gradually revived and revitalized in this Christian community. This is a practice worthy of emulation by all families, churches, communities and social organizations which together make up a city.

Your Reading Habit:

A recent survey disclosed that a great percentage of an average city's population are no longer keen on reading; and at the rate people are losing their reading habits, it is feared that by the next decade, or so, some bookshops and libraries may have to shut down.

It is not my intention to delve into the statistics of this situation right here and now because it is obviously not an encouraging one. But suffice it to say that reading as a habit has remained the best form of ideas-imparter. The popular saying easily come to mind here, which says "…..if you stop reading, you soon stop communicating." And when we realize the importance of communication --- that even the entire universe was created by the potency of communication, then we should not under-rate the constant need to continue to improve upon our reading habits, so that we can always be involved in informed and creative communications, capable of changing lives and situations around us for the better.

It is interesting to observe that books and reading materials have in deed, survived the test of time, such that despite some mind-bogging scientific and technological breakthroughs in the field of learning, books and reading habits still occupy their unique place in the scheme of things. Yes, it is indeed amazing that innovations in the electronic media have not been able to render books useless and irrelevant. Think of it! Rather, newer and newer books are being written and published by the day; and libraries keep stocking volumes upon volumes, of both old and new books.

Use of other media can only be an extension of book volumes, but definitely not a substitute or replacement; and even then, books enjoy a longer lifespan than all those!

This issue therefore poses a great challenge to all the living, to not only cultivate their reading habits, but that existing readers should work hard to improve upon theirs. For instance, there are training programs that coach readers to learn to read faster and faster. Obviously, learning to read faster can enable a reader to consume many more volumes in a given time than would have been possible. Such programs are available in audio and videotapes. You can inquire from your local library or book- shop. Readers and intending readers could locate some local readers' club or association and enlist. The idea is to expose you to others engaged in the same pursuit; and it is not unlikely that when you go to such a place, you are exposed to those who are at different levels of competence; and you may discover that your aspirations are within easy-reach as you identify with them.

When you are there, you would definitely identify with your area of interest thereby serving as monitors and being conversant with the state of the art in this area and other related areas like public speaking.

If you try to compare some 18th Century ideologies with those of recent years, you would find a lot of changes that have taken place. Similarly, an inspiration you had yesterday, may already be outdated if placed within today's context; this also poses a challenge to everyone to keep constantly updating him- self, which is better achieved by reading. The challenge to the living remains to constantly keep pace with developing trends in culture, science and technology. And because the source is divine, the flow continues forever.

But here, you have to exercise some caution; reason being that once there is an idea that is good, some contending forces will sooner or later come up with their counterfeits! This places an additional responsibility to everyone in their areas of specialization. It should be noted that while the source of all good ideas is God, equally the source of bad or counterfeit ideas is the devil. So when it comes to choosing what to read, what is it that catches your fancy? Some are attracted by topical materials, others prefer to read character books, while some like some- thing that can excite them such as movies, animal kingdom or other exciting materials.

Before, you proceed, you should determine in your heart, the direction you wish to go. But in my opinion, when you decide to read, don't spend precious time on a light weight material, or materials that will not contribute academically to your knowledge bank. And by that I mean, stuff that will not actually worth the time you put into reading them. Obviously, reading a bad stuff would be worse than no reading at all, if it gives rise to inordinate behavior or excesses. A good guide to your reading selection, is identifying your grade level in school and of course your moral persuasion. So, it is important that you know at the end of the day, what you expect to get from your reading exercise before you embark on the expedition!

Reading habit is difficult to cultivate initially; but once you successfully make a start, you discover that it is an indispensable hobby. For instance, how often you hear people say "Reading market a man!" And that is true; but you cannot actualize the truth in this saying unless you know how to make a good selection of what to read. You've got to be sure of what you are looking for before you set out to read.

Personally, when I want to read, I go looking out for highly researched materials, that will keep me informed or updated about the latest in current affairs, science and technology. Another write up that attracts my attention are books on highly principled, respected and successful individuals, etc.; so that at the end of the exercise, my reading would make an addition to the quality of my lifestyle and of course, knowledge.

I love some gentlemen, who assign themselves one book that must go along with a particular business trip or vacation as a task; so what do you find? Whether in a jet plane, a bus or a taxi, they fill up any available free moment with the book on

hand. Invariably, by the time the trip is over, that book is thoroughly perused. And before you know it, this person is adopting an improved way of doing things or a change of lifestyle.

Like some, you may say, "I'll watch the television movies and that will be enough!" Others would say "Let me watch those who read, and learn from their lifestyle!" Well, let me tell you, you can never learn enough watching others perform from what they read; no matter how hard you try!

There are certain critical ideas that you would have to extract by yourself. That is to say, there can be no alternative to digging out the facts yourself. The apparent challenge for every- one here therefore, is that to get the best out of life, you should strive to strike a balance of lifestyle by having a proportionate intake of every bit of good things that nature provides at your disposal; but not one at the expense of the other!

Needless state that in the area of reading, so much have indeed been compromised in modern times of scientific and technological advancements such that you begin to wonder whether such innovations are actually a blessing or a curse! This is because, most people have almost completely replaced their reading habits with DVD movies and other internet pro- grams of one kind or the other. But I put it to you, that this is not in your long-term interest!

What do you think makes the difference when you listen to some speak? Of course it is the contents of their hearts. Once they are well-fed with the right stuff, then when they speak, they communicate live to the hearers. But go to listen to anyone who is empty, the difference will simply be clear instantly! The reason is simple: You cannot give what you do not have! I would challenge you to show me one ideas man, who is not a reader, and I will readily show you many readers, who are ideas men! You may have heard the saying that "Readers become leaders, and therefore, leaders must be readers." Yet the reading habit is the one activity that is least practiced by leaders of tomorrow.

For the purpose of this article, we shall be using inter- changeably, the terms: appetite, potential, and habit as the text might demand but all in all they are meant to help drive the same point home! Never you desire to develop your potentials in a lopsided manner, because the potentials you develop, eventually consumes your whole being; and they all start at the point of thought-conception. For instance, experience has shown that most things we wish for ourselves, do come to pass or become a reality in course of time, especially when we deliberately work towards them as a goal. When you set up a goal for yourself, before you know it, your whole being has started agitating to actualize that wish. For instance, most people conceive an idea in their mind, and eventually put efforts into gear, and in course of time, such a dream becomes a reality.

As a result of a particular dream, some have eventually become nurses, or doctors, or engineers, etc. Thus, as important as this achievement may be, towards earning a livelihood, you discover that once you are at this point which you thought was an end in itself, you come to realize that it is only yet a means to another end, as it hardly gives you the desired fulfillment; especially when you bring into focus, the issue of fulfilling your life's destiny!

There and then, you get to realize that some of the things you thought to be so important previously are no more that important; instead those things you thought were not so important, like your chore habits of reading novels and perhaps writing and sharing and interacting with people, have become overwhelmingly, the more important issue of your life! This scenario explains why you often find many high professionals become preachers, TV evangelists, which is totally outside of their area of specialization.

So what point are we driving at here? Simply to say that developing your appetite for reading and doing a few extra-curricular activities can open the door for you to realize your life's destiny, and to operate at a much higher plane than would have been possible in your profession.

Suffice it to say that becoming a habitual reader, is capable of exposing you to world of ideas firstly from a local point of view and graduating to a nation, international or global perspectives, until you begin to see things from a spiritual perspective

The covenant people of contemporary times

Definitely there is a level you reach, God would open your eyes to begin to see things in the light of the blue print of the Master Architect Himself; and at that level, you'd see that of all man's achievements, only God should be given the glory; as man is at best, merely rediscovering what has already been in place.

No wonder the bible says that *it is He who gives you power to make wealth* (Deut.8 verse 18). You may perhaps begin to see why Simon Peter of the Bible and his colleagues, James and John the sons of Zebedee decided to quit their fishing jobs, despite their momentary extra-ordinary exploits, to follow JESUS! (Luke 5: 9-11).

As you begin to get appetized with good reading materials like your Bible, for instance I could foresee your spiritual eyes suddenly sprout wide open to behold HIM! And when that hap- pens, you too would probably quit your old ideas, concepts and conceptualizations about life, and fully adopt that of JESUS; and of course, you will no more be the same any more. May that be your experience as you read through this material, in Jesus Name (Amen).

MAKING UP YOUR MIND TO READ:

The covenant people of contemporary times

So, how can we begin to develop the habit of reading now, in view of the magnitude of its importance to our very existence here? Well, my response to that question is that first of all, you should make up your mind to become a reader by adopting the reading habit as a hobby in every sense of the word. Then, pray to God to help you develop your reading potentials, so that you can make positive impact on the lives of people. When you believe that your prayer has been answered, then make a selection of what to read. There are lots of good books in most book-shops to choose from.

Don't just read anything in the name of seeking an appetite for reading! Rather, be selective of what you read henceforth. I would suggest you get yourself, a modern version of the Holy Bible. That is the version you can read and easily understand what it is saying. You should please take time to follow my prescription of a constructive type of reading here by beginning again with the Holy Bible and watch the difference this new approach will make in your life.

By the way, I'm sure you know that all the professional disciplines that be, got their inspirations from the Scriptures Then you can go ahead and get some good Christian literatures on specific topics; you can also get some biography and autobiography books. Make a topical selection that deal with specific areas that will be of benefit to you personally. Note the watchword is "Be Selective." Buy books that you would love to read.

Another point to be considered is the environment. You see, life here, and in other parts of the world are so demanding, that the average individual has little or no leisure time to himself. Invariably though, you may find some, who in an attempt to maximize their earning potential, keep two or three jobs at a time. It is so serious that they can't even find time to go to church, nor to spend time with their families (children, husbands or wives!) Suffice it to say once your objectives are defined and vigorously pursued, you'll find everything fitting into their proper perspectives. One thing you should realize is that the end product of a properly managed time is a " balanced personality!"

However, if you find that your entire life and personality has no balance or meaning, even though you use all your time to make money, you may discover that this might be a clear indication that you are not having a balanced intake of nature's bounties and of course, this might constitute a red signal that a change is necessary! That is to say, if you form the desirable habit of reading different views expressed in books and magazines etc., you won't need anyone to tell you to make some necessary adjustments in your life. In other words, a balanced and enhanced lifestyle will be a matter of course.

To buttress my point, this author has had the opportunity of working as a Customer Service representative. This job required the staff sitting up in service booths and attending to costumers' demands and inquires for the duration of each shift. Under such an environment, reading any written material would appear to be impracticable. But having worked hard on my reading habit, I could not just do away with it now; this is because, among other things, I had to keep myself constantly informed despite the pressure of the job on hand, I had to find time convenient (or inconvenient) to read my book. You ask how, and my answer is that in any work situation, there is always a peak time, and periods of low pressure. There is never a job where you would work non-stop for eight hours or whatever number of hours you wish to work for the day. In addition to that, there must also be a break time of at least thirty minutes to one hour.

And during such times, what you do with your time is a matter of choice! You can play away the precious time, or use it to look into your any pet activity, or book; that is if you are a reader!

That way, little by little, you can go through one or two choice books in a week; and with the ideas you accumulate, your reasoning faculty is further sharpened. And you find that you are better informed than most of your counterparts. To assist you in achieving this, you should ensure that you make a good selection. Secondly, such a book should be bag, or pocket friendly. That is to say, by its size, it should be able to conveniently go into your hand-bag, or pocket. Most modern books are deliberately made quite handy. The idea is to enable you to take it along with you, while on tour, at work, or elsewhere, so that reading continuity can be maintained. Obviously however, not everybody can afford the luxury of spending quality-time in the privacy of their study room, or perhaps at public libraries; but nevertheless, the lifestyle of reading must be maintained. Just as other aspects of living cannot be suspended nor ignored, for any reason! Also, I once had a memorable opportunity of working with a " blind" Evangelist. Although, this man had a physical handicap associated with the eyes, yet he is somebody widely awake in the spirit. Here is a man who has insatiable appetite for reading, and of course, a man of great literary ideas! He met his basic needs for reading through braille literatures mailed to him on a regular basis. But because that appears not to be enough, he still engages his Personal Assistant (which rare position, this author had the privilege to occupy for three years) to read to him other selected conventional materials, like newspapers, magazines etc. Little wonder, that when he communicates, he simply imparts life-giving words and ideas to the listeners; and people often flock at his house and office for wise counsel. If you have been to ABU Teaching Hospital, in Zaria, Nigeria, then you will know the man I'm talking about. It is amazing! So if such a handicap could not stop a man like that from exercising his literary capabilities, then I don't see why you should not make a positive move to read, despite your own handicap, or the absence of it!

The point I am making here is very clear: If you, indeed stop reading, or you allow your reading habit to die a natural death, you should bear in mind that you won't go scot-free! Of course, the inevitable consequence is that you will eventually stop being able to communicate effectively. You might well be talking like every other average human being; but to effectively impart ideas onto others, will be a difficult task!

Another important reason is that God has endowed in you at least one or two important talents or gifts; and talents are normally given, so that they can be identified, developed, and utilized for the benefit of mankind. No matter how busy or unimportant you think you are, you have a responsibility to perform to the up-coming generation. And that is the intention of the Creator, who made you. That is to say, you are never made only to be self-serving; rather, you are made to be an instrument of blessing in the hand of the Creator. And to achieve this purpose easily and better, you must be a reader; and to be a reader, you must be prepared to develop the habit of reading!

CHOOSE YOUR READING MATERIAL:

As has been emphasized in the foregoing paragraphs, that to enjoy your reading habit, you need to be quite selective of what you spend your time reading! You don't just lay your hands on any stuff for the purpose of reading, neither should you spend your valuable time on materials that have little or nothing to offer you. So, to make the most from your reading time, take time to select the next book to explore, which is more likely to add something new to your awareness level, and more importantly, change your lifestyle one way or the other. Some people lay hands on any material they come across and start "wasting their time" on them. You should always read through the synopsis of any book at the back of the book to enable you to decide whether it is worth your time reading. This is necessary, because in a busy society like ours, time is money. The irony is that time is one commodity that everyone has an equal share of; yet some make a lot more out of their own share of time than others. This calls for wisdom.

But suffice it to say that, after you have had your morning devotion, the next thing you should do is to think of how you'd spend your own share of the 24 hours of the day. Plan how much time you should spend on one activity. If that is difficult, then list out a few important things you'd like to accomplish in a given day. At the end of the day, try and evaluate how your plans has worked out. You may then be able to see areas that will need

improvement, so that you'd do even better the next day. When the Scripture exhorts us to number our days, so that we will apply our hearts to wisdom it is telling us among other things, to learn how we utilize our time; but we are not to spend time, but rather to invest in it.

So when we talk of being choosy in what you read, time is an important factor to consider. That means you should ensure that by so doing, such time in reading , is actually an investment that can affect your life positively for the rest of your years on earth. You should therefore read to keep yourself informed. You should read also, to educate yourself concerning specific topics or issues that make you better informed.

However, if you have difficulty in choosing what to read, then your problem is quite simple. Why, because, you can easily lay hands on one book that covers all areas of learning. We mentioned a book like this earlier. Once you have this book in your handbag, or pocket, then you can read up everything concerning anything that makes for life and godliness: and you will discover for yourself, that it is indeed, the Book of books. This book has different versions to it, and comes in different sizes. This book, as portable and handy as it is, has as many as sixty- six books in one. It speaks the mind of God, and the mind of men. It tells you the whole lot about life and character of godly and successful people in comparison to those of ungodly and of course, unsuccessful people! It tells us what it means to be successful in life. It also tells you about God's plan for your life. It tells you about life on earth and life hereafter.

It tells you how the universe was made and how of all the nine planets of the universe, planet earth is the center of God's attraction, because mankind whom He made in his own image inhabit it. Yet, we do know that what we know as the center of attraction amongst other planets, is neither so magnificent nor the most beautiful in its features!

Well, you may say it is most beautiful, since it accommodates mankind, the crown of God's creation. Well, from a little research I carried out, I discovered that the earth was simply placed third in sequence to the sun, so there will just be enough warmth to sustain life on the planet. If it had been closer than that, then it would have been too hot and therefore uninhabitable. It was not placed too far from the sun either, else it would have been too cold to live in.

Furthermore, my research of the solar system, reveals that of all the nine planets that exist, namely, Mercury, Venus, then Earth, Mars, Jupiter, Saturn, Uranus, Neptune, and Pluto, it is only Planet Earth, as far as we know, that supports life, and living, (despite of ongoing research on Mars capability in this regard.) The nine planets are so arranged in such an order that they take turns to orbit the sun, which supplies warmth to all of God's Creation. That means, the Sun, was placed at the center of the solar system, and all other planets rotate around it at varying speeds and at different altitudes, such that no one will clash into another! What a wonderful arrangement by a Great God! And while it takes planet earth 24 hours to orbit the sun, it takes planets such as Uranus, the 7th in sequence to the sun, 84 years, and Pluto, the 9th takes 248 years to do the process. From the varying circumstances surrounding these planets, you could see why no life exits there, because they would either be too hot, or too cold at any given time.

You should also remember that apart from these nine planets, there are other elements that orbit the solar system, known as asteroids. This particular factor makes me to wonder sometimes, when people talk of unknown foreign objects (ufos) that operate in space and destroy spaceships and aircrafts. Now, do you know that these include rocks, some as large as 600 miles in diameter that orbit the sun? Think of this friend! You may also have known that of all the earth's surface, man inhabits only about 30 per cent of it. The rest 70 per cent is occupied by water i.e. the oceans, the high and low seas and rivers!

Now, back to the solar system: Do you know that the sun is about one million times the size of planet earth (i.. e. 1sun = 1m x earth size). Similarly, Jupiter is three times larger than the earth.

Friend, there is a whole lot than can startle your imagination concerning the wonders of creation. Yet in all these wonders, man, the crown of God's creation inhabits only 30 per cent of earth's land space, the 3rd planet from the sun. From this brief study of the solar system you can imagine how Great, our God is; you probably can also imagine how important you are to Him; why therefore you cannot afford to toy with the wonderful opportunities He gives you to affect your immediate environment for him; and that is why you should in deed, study to show yourself, approved unto Him, so that you can indeed, be a useful work man for Him!

It may not be out of place to pause now, and sing the well-known "Oh Lord My God" song. Shall we now go:-

> *Oh Lord my God, when I in awesome wonder*
> *Consider all, the works thy hands hath made*
> *I see the stars, I hear the roaring thunder*
> *That spread throughout, the universe thou hast made*
>
> *Then sings my soul, My Savior God to*
> *thee) How Great thou art, How Great thou*
> *art!) x2*

You may begin to wonder at the relevance of this song to the subject topic; if that is the case, I would tell you that it is all about inspiration! As you take to reading as a habit, or you try to work hard to improve yours, you will begin to draw a lot of inspiration from what you read, such that occasionally, there'll be outburst of songs, so copious that if written down, will fill up many pages.

Perhaps you know a number of Song Books that exist. Most of them are products of inspirations from God; and as you know, it is never on any record book that the existing

Song books are the only ones that will ever be written. So who knows, perhaps you'll be the next popular songwriter of the century, or one of the great innovative writers that can be.

Be that as it may, the chances of this happening may be very rare unless you take to reading as a habit.

Needless say that if you begin to have recourse to the wise writings of old, and that of contemporary times, you will invariably become wise yourself? No two ways about it! For instance, the Scripture has this to say in Psalms 19:

"The Law of the Lord is perfect, converting the soul; The Testimony of the Lord is sure, making wise the simple. The Statutes of the Lord is clean, enduring forever, the Judgment of the Lord is pure, enlightening the eyes. The fear of the Lord is clean, enduring forever; the Judgments of the Lord are true, and righteous altogether. More to be desired are they than gold, yea, than much fine gold; Sweeter also than honey, and the honeycomb. Moreover, by them is thy servant warned; and in keeping them there is great reward." (vv. 7-11).

Oh friend, there is a lot of Scriptures you can search out for yourself that is relevant to the subject matter. All you need do is to program yourself to read, and/or to improve your reading habits. The Psalmist must have considered some of these facts when he penned down these psalms. Awed by his awareness of the Almighty God, David further penned down the following:

"O LORD our Lord, how majestic is your name in all the earth! You have set your glory above the heavens. From the lips of children and infants, you have ordained praise because of your enemies, to silence the foe and the avenger. When I consider your heavens, the work of your fingers, the moon and stars, which you have set in place, what is man that you are mindful of him; and the son of man that you care for him? Yet you have made him a little lower than the

heavenly beings and crowned him with glory and honor. You made him ruler over the works of your hands. You put everything under his feet: all flocks and herds, and the beasts of the field, the birds of air and the fish of the sea. All that swim the path of the seas. Oh Lord our Lord, how majestic is your Name in all the earth! (Psalm 8) (NIV).

That is it! Most readers speak and write from inspiration they received from God. Do you know that reading can be an oral form of research? In the academic arena, for instance, in order for you to make progress in any chosen field, you must be a researcher in order to discover new trends in the field. In general too, you must be convincingly knowledgeable in your chosen area, in order for you to be able to make any reasonable impact on society; and this is where you will find information gathering through the process of reading very important. In that case, some magazines and journals of international repute, can be quite useful.

These magazines carry highly researched materials on science and technology, management sciences, politics and business management generally. Some of them include The Readers Digest, Time magazine, Newsweek, *News watch* magazines, you name them! You can subscribe to some of them that you really find quite educative. You'd find that you pay less when you subscribe than when you are a piecemeal buyer or reader; because often you are entitled to subscribers' discounts. Reading as a hobby is therefore, not a novelty but a time-tested beneficial phenomenon which provides you a self-driven ladder to success!

The problem of lack of readership ironically, a global phenomenon but on a serious note, if you choose not to develop your reading habit, then you are unwittingly making yourself a slave to the world of ignorance. And that will be a 21st century type of slavery! The choice is yours!

READING FROM THE BIBLE:

We have so far looked at reading from a general point of view; and being a Bible-based motivational book, we should now try to locate our reading habits within the context of the Bible. The book called The Bible is a unique book, often referred to as "The Book of Books" because it is a precedent to all fields of endeavor, and all areas of learning. It is the only book that is inspired by God, compiled by 40 authors over a period of 1600 years. Until recently, some of the ancient scripts that form part of the Bible are still being discovered; so that some who previously did not believe in the uniqueness of the Bible are changing their minds!

More than that, it is the only book that tells you about how life came about here on Planet Earth; how the life can be successfully lived; how to experience the love of God, and how to live for God; and how one can live with God hereafter. The Bible is the only book that is self-interpreting and self-explaining. It is made up of 66 Books, with the Old Testament constituting 39 books and the New Testament, 27 books. The Bible is available in different sizes to fit your hand bag or pockets. It is one of God's best gifts to man. Some who know the value of the Bible, call it Life Manual! But I think it is more than that!

Now once your reading habit is fully developed, you can plan to read through the entire Bible in one year. As a matter of fact, you should not wait for your reading habit to improve before you start with your Bible. Rather, you should practice reading with your Bible as part of the exercise. If you do, you would end up achieving a dual purpose success: Firstly, you would improve your reading habit, and secondly, you would educate and edify yourself.

Getting accustomed to your Bible will enable you to grasp God's concept of creation, and the role you and other creatures of God are expected to play in the scheme of things. You would also discover how it is, that man is the crown of God's creation, and more than that, how it is that God is keenly interested in the affairs of men.

If reading through the Bible is the desire of your heart, here is a suggested way you can inspire yourself towards achieving such a noble objective. Now, imagine that you have a loved one living in a far-away country. You have been hoping and dreaming of a day, when you can be reunited together. All of a sudden, the day arrives, and your loved one sent you a very long letter, (20 pages perhaps), describing how this trip would be made, and telling you about the wonderful prospects that await you. Imagine what your reaction will be when you receive such a letter. Needless state that you would read, and read, and read, and would not wish to drop this letter until you have read through it non-stop, and perhaps re-read it again!

Obviously such a letter would arouse your curiosity so much so that you won't want to pay a partial attention to it. Definitely, every other thing would have to wait until you are done reading this 'precious letter' from your loved one. Friend, that should be your attitude to this love manual we received from God, called the Bible, that contains all the wonderful news about your life here, what will become of you hereafter that you can ever imagine. Once you develop this frame of mind, then I believe you would cherish reading your Bible. For instance, if your Bible teacher asks you to read one chapter a day, you would even want to exceed that many times over!

Having said that, you should be ready to read at least, three chapters a day per reading session, if your aim is to read through this book in a calendar year; and like the love letter described above, with that kind of attitude, you would find that you could even far exceed this minimum thereby getting the job done in good record time!

Perhaps this little testimony may help to drive home my point: When I got born again many years ago and I bought my first complete Holy Bible, the hunger for the Word was so much in me that I virtually 'consumed' it like someone who had lost a lot of time! So within me, burned the desire to discover the plan of God for my life, so that I might obey and continue to be safe in Him! You might not quite appreciate what I am trying to explain here, neither do I expect you to do exactly what I did; but definitely, the desire to be godly and to know the mind of God should be upper most in every body's heart and mind. And with such a desire there, you can easily make a success of your Bible study exercise! Another thing that might be of help to you, is to learn to follow the footsteps of previous successful explorers of the Word of God, by taking advantage of their remarkable discoveries and practical examples from their books.

However, Saint John's Gospel provides us with an introductory approach to the Bible because it starts with God's plan of salvation for all men, as fulfilled in the death and resurrection of His only begotten Son, Jesus Christ. After that, you can take on the Book of Luke's Gospel, who had a knack for details --- probably because of his academic approach in his writing, being a medical practitioner. Then take on Matthew, and then Mark. You should of course, bear in mind that these four authors are giving the account of the same event as they saw it from their different perspectives, and they are known as the synoptic gospels. The four components should therefore make up one complete salvation story, or God's Visitation to Planet Earth! Usually, where one missed, the other covered up, and in most cases each one retold the story of the same event. An issue of much more importance, is to see where the message applies to you personally.

After the gospels, you can then go on to read the account of the early church, in the Acts of the Holy Spirit, popularly known as the Acts of the Apostles; followed by the Epistles of Saint Paul during his missionary journeys to some parts of Africa and Asia Minor. You may attempt the Book of Revelation much later, after you got your bearings right with the other books. You may then go on to Genesis and read up the creation story and the fall of man. After these, you can then adopt a topical approach. All in all, the main idea should be to get something tangible from your study sessions as opposed to a mere newspaper-approach reading exercise.

At this stage, you might find it necessary to either accelerate your pace or to slow down depending on your rate of comprehension. To get the best out of your study sessions, always shut yourself out from distractions, depending on what constitutes a distraction to you. Have a notebook and a pen with you to jot down any new message that you receive from your study session, as well as any questions that may emanate therefrom. You could seek further clarifications from your Bible Study Teacher or your Pastor if necessary. The foregoing procedure is only a guide to making your study session successful and rewarding.

However, if you follow this procedure, you will enjoy a very rewarding experience exploring your Bible aimed at helping you discover who you really are within the context of God's Covenant.

CHAPTER TWELVE

BENEFITS OF A SOUND READING HABIT

We have deliberately devoted quite some time on 'Studying to Understand the Bible' in the previous chapter. The simple reason is that it is a 'book of books,' as you may have already observed. Even if you make a good selection of other reading materials successfully, you'll discover that you still need the Bible. And for you to meet up with all the volume of materials that need to be read plus your Book of books, then your reading habit really needs to be developed or improved upon. It is very necessary if your wish is to actualize your life's dreams, and in effect, your destiny. I mean, if reading were not important, there would be no necessity for God Himself to emphasize to Moses and

The covenant people of contemporary times

Joshua, the need to peruse and meditate on the Scriptures, in order to actualize not just a successful leadership pattern, but a very good one! (See Joshua 1:8, ff).

We shall now pause to take a look at the benefits you can derive as you develop a sound reading habit. Some of the benefits you stand to derive by learning to read are too numerous to mention. If you should pay a visit to some developed countries and some developing ones, like USA, Europe, Africa, Brazil, to name a few, you will discover that at every nook and corner, there is a great deal of papers circulating in the form of newspapers, news magazines, brochures and handbills etc. Most of these papers are distributed or made available, free of charge.

This is commonplace in countries like USA, Europe and other industrialized States. People are even begged to collect these papers and just read. They do this, not because it does not cost money to run these papers off the press! Instead, the reason is that these papers, by whatever name they are called, contain some important information, which they intend to pass on to people and of course, to be among this target category of people, you must be a reader; otherwise, you would attach no importance to these papers.

You could now see why readers find fun, packing as much of these materials as they want, free of charge, just to keep themselves informed! So this is an added bonus for all those who have developed their faculties as readers. Readers are very often abreast with current affairs both locally and internationally because they read far and wide. To a non-reader, packing newspapers and taking them home could amount to packing trash into the house this is because, these heaps of papers constitute a nuisance; yet people with such views are the most ignorant set of people in town! Most non-readers depend solely on the radio and television for their information; but we know that the newspapers are exclusive in news coverage and permanence of record and easy reference.

Sociology teaches us that when one country has access to other cultures of the world it gives rise to a social change. For instance, the obnoxious trans-Atlantic slave trade of the 18th and 19th centuries created a new social order - the African American nation, some of who have not been able to trace their primary root in Africa till today! And even those who have, could hardly settle down in their former social order neither could they, in the other extreme. Consequently, they have to settle in a totally new social order because they find themselves neither here nor there, due to no fault of theirs! Be that as it may, if you are in that category, I have good news for you that may gladden your heart: From my own humble reading habit, and study of the books, it has become quite clear that what differentiates one race from the other is merely color, language and culture, which are of course, terrestrial and temporal.

Naturally, nobody has a black, blue, yellow or pink blood but every normal person's blood has the color of red, irrespective of the person's color, language or culture. Another man-made thing that differentiates mankind is cosmopolitan law. For instance, there is usually certain features that make the law of the land of a particular country different from that of others due mainly to the circumstances of their history. But there is one law that is universal: and that is the SPIRITUAL LAWS; or the Laws of God.

The same spiritual laws are binding on every living being (i.e. human beings, not beasts). That law stipulates among other things, that "The soul that sinneth shall die." And no matter who you are, this law is equally applicable to you. It also states that "Whatever a man sows, that shall he also reap." It also says ""Do unto others as you would have them do unto you." The Law also says " Love your neighbor as yourself." So from these little tips of the Spiritual Laws, you could see that spiritually, many are already walking in spiritual condemnation, because they have exceedingly contravened the law of God.

And this situation brings us to the question of being born again. As you would agree, a spiritual problem requires a spiritual solution (q.e.d.) From my reading habit, and study of books so far, only the Christian Manual also called the Holy Bible provides solution to such spiritual problems, in such a way that somebody who is spiritually condemned can have another chance to begin life again; and it refers to such experience as being born again. But before you can be given the spiritual power and status to begin life again, you must first of all show signs of a change of heart, which is generally referred to as repentance. Here, Jesus was addressing his audience over people who were punished for walking under spiritual condemnation like the present case, and He paused to tell them this truth:

"I tell you, no! But unless you repent, you too will all perish." (Luke 13:3)

In another scenario, one prominent man came forward to express his amazement over the miraculous works which Jesus performed.

And it appeared like Jesus put it straight back to him, to stop getting too excited about my miracles! But then, went on to draw the man's attention to a more critical issue: the poor state of the man's spiritual condition. Let's read about it:

" ….Jesus answered and said unto him, Verily, verily, I say unto thee, except a man be born again, he cannot see the kingdom of God" (John 3:3)

The sum total of the dialogue that ensued after Jesus' injunction was in Nicodemus' inquiry as to how he, being a full-fledged old man, can still have the privilege of being born again. And I shall go ahead and tell you about it in a nutshell so that you may take advantage of it right away! But definitely, as you begin your reading expedition, I would suggest you read through that interesting dialogue in St. John's Gospel, Chapter 3 yourself.

Now also, as stated above, to be born again and freed from spiritual condemnation, requires that you show a change of heart. Tell God how sorry you are about your sins and transgressions. Tell Him to give you another chance to make things right, promising to live for Him if you could have such a chance.

If you say all that sincerely from your heart, then rest assured that God will hear you and forgive you accordingly. I say this because the Bible confirms that

God looks at the thoughts and intentions of the heart, and not necessarily on the outward appearance of man! So the next step you should take after that, is to invite Jesus Christ into your life, as your Lord and Savior. Tell Him to give you the power to be His child from today. Religious practices alone, cannot achieve what this prayer will for you; no matter how hard you try! So if you followed this prescribed steps, you will definitely experience the miracle of forgiveness; and the peace of mind that will result in you, will even confirm this to you.

In St. John's Gospel, 1:12, the Bible says as follows:

"But as many as received Him, to them gave He power to become the sons of God, even to them that believe on His Name."

So friend, I think this is the most important section of this booklet. The reason is because, once you become a child of God and receive the power of adoption, then the power to be a reader will equally result; because the Power of God you receive subsequent to your rebirth, will enable you to achieve anything that make for life and godliness quite easy, and save you from a poor life of struggles! The power to do anything worthwhile comes only form above (from God of course). So Congratulations!

The phenomenon of social change surmises to say that 'the greater the access we have to other cultures, the greater the social change that is likely to occur.' To experience the much-needed change in social orientation, either through the acquisition of the 'golden fleece' or other attainments of value, you may have traveled several hundreds of miles away from home, with all manners of attendant risks. Although often we hear that traveling is part of education, which may be quite credible, but oftentimes you may wish to undertake such trips, but for resources-constraints sake, you discover in reality that you cannot. In that case, what do you do? Give up your dream? Never! Of course, the real answer is the subject topic of our discussion here --- Reading. Reading can be the answer, if you have already cultivated the habit. You can thus educate yourself even from your room, if you are a reader; similarly, you can travel round the world while staying in your room, if you can but read. Also, you can become acquainted with the cultures of the world, through reading.

Reading also sharpens vision, as opposed to being a habitual television watcher. You see, the television tends to have the opposite effect upon your vision as reading. And of course, when you read, you are equally exercising the full potentials of your eyesight, just like you exercise your natural physique when you do a bodily exercise. Also, when you develop the habit of reading your Bible, I believe the spiritual power in the Word of God, does a lot of good things to your entire system; including healing, edification, and enlightenment. Try it!

As you begin to advance in your reading expedition, you would discover the need to program yourself vis-à-vis available time toward reaching the goal you have set for yourself. As stated earlier, choose topical books and align them to your overall objective. It might not be possible to sit all day reading only one particular subject matter; and that spells the need to program yourself. Even if watching the television is your hobby equally, you should always be selective of what you watch, making sure that after spending the allotted time to watching a particular program, such a time would not be a wasted one for you by reason of what you realize from the exercise.

Of course there is a lot of fringe benefits you derive when you sharpen your reading habits. I had already stated that of sharpening your eyesight. For instance, in the Bible, when Moses was age 120 years, and yet his physique as well as his visionary abilities did not abate. (Deut. 34:7). This is indeed typical of a man who really exercised his God-given faculties on a continual basis and for God's Service. Some therefore define themselves as members of "Moses Company" or perhaps "Caleb's Company!" Which one are you identifying with?

Also, quite often, you hear of people who are said to be retired, but not tired. Any time you hear of such statements, make no mistake about it. It is not talking of old men who are physically strong, or demonstrate some physical prowess despite their age. No! Instead such statements more often than not, is referring to people who though aged, but still demonstrate their mental alacrity because their ideas are still fresh and current! And I put it to you that any time you find such men, go close to them and you will discover that they were, or are habitual readers.

Take time out to pay a casual visit to any good bookstore in town; and what you'll discover will amaze you. Because you will find that some you think are too old, still frequent there, to see what is the latest on the book shelf, to nurture their reading appetites. This is possible because, to them it has become a lifestyle, and you cannot afford to be outdated.

To a great majority of people, who are not used to reading, it may appear out of place to think of visiting the library or bookshops. Some youths can't even imagine what is good at such places.

Yet suffice it to say that such places they seem to ignore, is a place in the real sense, that are laboratories of truth and life, the repository of materials that can make a total man; materials indeed, that can make you a very useful member of society.

From the sum of the foregoing you could see that developing your reading appetite is one of the essentials for good living capable also, of making you in course of time, a possessor of great spiritual and literary ideas, and an imparter of life to all 'the lifeless beings' that walk around you on account of lack of knowledge!

LEAVING A LEGACY:

The use of the word "legacy" as important a legal term it is, has so often been misused and misapplied in recent times, so much so that oftentimes, some are reluctant to apply it in figures of speech or writing style. Sometimes you find yourself better understood when you talk primarily of living and leaving an exemplary lifestyle. In all you do in life, you should always realize that you are unwittingly making an impression on someone else's life. Such a person may be your child, your friend, relation or even someone that may not be closely related to you. So, never you go with the impression that you are living only for yourself ok? Never! Once you get this settled in your mind, then you would know that you should leave no stone unturned in making your life count anywhere you find yourself; because at any given time, there is always the necessity to leave a good impression behind you (pro tem or lifetime legacy); and so try to make it a point of duty to see that the impression you leave behind, anywhere you go, or function, is a good one. It goes without saying that once you develop your appetite for reading, you have become an icon in society; because you would not consider anything too big or too little to evaluate. Instead, you'll have a broad-hearted value-interest in a wide variety of human activities.

Though some may call you names, like "bookworms," "paper addicts," etc. You don't listen to them. In any case, you don't expect men to call you good names when you are desperately pursuing a goal. At an advanced form, you become a self- made editor, orator, writer, you name it; why, because, you have acquainted yourself thoroughly in the theories and practices of most areas of human endeavor. And nothing makes a man fulfilled in life like achieving your life's goal, and being able to make a positive impact in your environment. Once you achieve that, then the issue of legacy or leaving a good example are already taken care of because the impact of who you are is already being felt in society.

Having said that, I challenge you to go back to your book- shelf, or wherever you left your books, get them dusted up and commence the art of reading once again! If you have forgotten how to make a start, then find a local adult class in your neighborhood or at the appropriate website on the internet, and in no distant time, you'd find yourself reading again. There is always a way out of any problem so long as you can persevere and search for it like a missing treasure!

Finally, you should constantly evaluate your capability in the light of the following maxims: "Readers are leaders! Am I a reader?" "Reading makes a man! Can I now call myself a man?" "If you stop reading, you stop communicating! Can I really communicate an idea effectively?" Etc. The challenges that some of these self-questions may pose, will definitely prod you into further action. And whatever you do to improve your reading appetite, do not leave out reading your Bible, the book of books!

Blessings!

** Supplementary Reading to Chapter Five.

EPILOGUE

This hand book is an inspirational, and motivational reading material meant to inspire and challenge every believer in Christ primarily, as well as those who are yet to believe, to begin to discover the mysteries of godliness in Christ, who alone symbolizes God's effort to reach and reconcile man with the realities of godliness, as opposed to centuries-old man's futile efforts to reach God, in other words known as Religion! Christianity has to do with relationship with one another, and God, in the symbolic "Cross" format. Man may continue to be passive about Issues of the Covenant for as long as he has the time! But it is also important to realize that God's permissive will, will not last forever; so everyone should learn to 'make the hay, while the sun shines,' as it were! This book also challenges everyone to bear their cross through a lifestyle of prevailing prayer, and showing forth the light, through manifest godly character, (the fruit of the Holy Spirit); and in so doing, make a difference in the lives of people we come across at different walks of life, both at our immediate and remote environments.

It highlights the fact that the world now seems more interested in seeing what makes you different from the rest of humanity! Apparently they have heard and seen enough of professed religion, but now expect only to see those who actually "possess," as opposed to those who merely "profess" the character of God! In other words, everyone is now looking out to see those who are by practice and character, the manifest sons of God!

This book also brings to mind, the fact that for every opportunity a believer loses in making this Godly impact, the devil seems to take a greater advantage! And we know that the devil's own mission is simply to kill, to steal and to destroy! But God's remains "...to give life, and give it in abundance..."

This book therefore challenges all human creations of God, especially those called by His name in all walks of life, to wake up to their responsibilities wherever you are! For to do so means life and health, peace and longevity and of course, we all know that there can be no alternative to doing the will of God!

It is a recommended reading for all lovers of books, as a challenging inspirational reading material. It is also recommended as a Bible Study discussion material for both youths and adult classes.

OTHER TITLES IN CIRCULATION:

• Developing Appetite For Christian Diets.......

• The Covenant Man in Contemporary Times.....

• Fixing Your Real Issues Now.......

• The Tragedy of the Falling Stars......

• Team Players for a Worthy Goal......

• The Dividends of Faith......

• Making A Successful Trip to Africa.....

----------oOo----------

To Get Your Copy, Visit:
www.createspace.com/drnwoguguj@usa.com. Or get in touch with the author directly. God bless u!

READY TO LAUNCH:

"The COVENANT PEOPLE OF CONTEMPORARY TIMES"

You are cordially invited to be part of an epoch-making event, even the launching of an *earthshaking* book for everyone: "The Covenant People of Contemporary Times" as put together by a research scholar and friend, Dr. Johnny N. Celestine.

Indeed, it is expedient that you constantly for the habit of reading up the latest from "The Throne Room" as Servants of God continue to receive inspiration, and more importantly, as we see the signs of His Second Coming occur by the hours and minutes before our own eyes!

This book helps to define the Total Man & Woman within the context of God's Covenant. "When the going gets tough, the tough gets going" goes an old saying! And "Once an issue is defined, it is half-solved" goes another!! "To be forewarned, is to be forearmed" goes yet another!!!

The need to identify yourself within the context of "The Covenant" therefore, cannot be overemphasized at this point in time! While this is considered the best thing to do, yet the choice is absolutely yours!

Once you identify who you really are, then fulfilling your Covenant roles will follow naturally, it is strongly believed!! And of course, you and I have no options about being alive to our Covenant responsibilities in times like these! And that makes this book, "The Covenant People of Contemporary Times" a "must" read for everyone!!! Get Your Copy NOW, and perhaps gift copies for those you love! Bless You!

NOTES

Made in the USA
San Bernardino, CA
11 June 2016